Understanding the Venezuelan Revolution

UNDERSTANDING THE VENEZUELAN REVOLUTION

Hugo Chávez Talks to Marta Harnecker

TRANSLATED BY CHESA BOUDIN

MONTHLY REVIEW PRESS

New York

Library of Congress Cataloging-in-Publication Data

Chávez Frías, Hugo.
  Understanding the Venezuelan revolution : Hugo Chávez talks to
Marta Harnecker / by Hugo Chávez and Marta Harnecker.
     p. cm.
  Includes bibliographical references and index.
  ISBN 1-58367-128-5 (cloth) — ISBN 1-58367-127-7 (pbk.)
   1. Chávez Frías, Hugo—Interviews. 2. Venezuela—History—1974-
1999. 3. Venezuela—History—1999- . 4. Presidents—Venezuela
—Interviews.   I. Harnecker, Marta. II. Title.
F2328.52.C48A5 2005
987.06'42'092—dc22
  [B]
                                        2005024483

Photographs courtesy Prensa Presidencial

MONTHLY REVIEW PRESS
122 West 27th Street
New York, NY 10001
www.monthlyreview.org

Printed in Canada

10 9 8 7 6 5 4 3 2 1

Contents

Acknowledgments

TO ALL THOSE WHO MADE THIS BOOK POSSIBLE, especially those who transcribed the tapes—in Venezuela, Jorgina Eloisa Moya, Belkis Herrera, Clara Carrillo, Dayimar Sosa, and in Cuba, Hilda Betancourt. To Bertha Menéndez and Pavel Alemán who collaborated in the editing. To Rafael Vargas, who was always willing and able to ease my doubts. To those who read the various chapters and gave me their opinions. To Nelly and Omar who prepared the chronology, to Lorena who relieved me from so many chores so I could concentrate on this project. And to the entire team at the research center, Memoria Popular Latinoamericana, who, as always, supported me through it all.

Introduction

I CAME UP WITH THE IDEA of interviewing Venezuelan president Hugo Chávez Frías in April 2002. I had scheduled a tour through several Venezuelan states to give lectures based on my latest writings. How could I not take advantage of that occasion to interview the leader of the Venezuelan revolutionary process—a process so distorted by the international media and so little understood by left-wing and progressive sectors in South America and around the world? This distortion is not surprising since what is happening in Venezuela is a *sui generis* process that explodes preconceived schemes of revolutionary processes.

There are a few basic characteristics of this process that this collection of interviews draws out. First, the process began with Chávez's overwhelming victory in an electoral battle and continues advancing via government institutions in spite of all the challenges it faces from opponents. Second, it is led by a former member of the military who six years earlier—trying to overcome Venezuela's political crisis at that time—dared to organize a military coup against the Pérez regime. Third, it has been unable to eliminate corruption—one of its main calls for change. Fourth, it isn't led by a political vanguard party. Fifth, it is undefined ideologically because it doesn't assume Marxism as the guiding ideology of the process, but rather Bolívarianism.

This ideology doesn't speak of class struggles but of Latin American integration. It conceives of democracy as the political system that brings the maximum happiness to the people. It doesn't allow the military to direct its weapons against the people. And, perhaps most significantly, it warns, as Bolívar did in the 1820s, "the United States of North America is a country destined by providence to plague Latin America with miseries in the name of freedom." Sixth, serious economic transformations have yet to materialize and it loyally pays the foreign debt.

Bearing in mind all these characteristics, many people wonder if it is really a revolutionary process. But paradoxically, there would have been a counterrevolution without a revolution.

I proposed to President Chávez that we engage in a substantial interview, starting with the general doubts and criticisms that some on the left have raised to allow him to discuss the following topics: Why he chose an institutional route to revolutionary change; the reasons the military has such an important presence both in government bodies and in directing many of the main revolutionary tasks; the characteristics of this generation of the Venezuelan military that make it different from other Latin American armies; the historical relationships with the organized Left and their failures; the economic model he seeks to put forward and the reasons for so little progress in this area; the difficulties faced, the errors made; what he has learned through these years, and his perspective on the reactionary coup of April 11 and his return to Miraflores [the presidential administrative palace in Caracas].

My intention is for this interview to publicize the Venezuelan process and the enormous challenges it faces in trying to achieve profound social transformations through peaceful constitutional means, and to provide material for those who—in the face of the savage neoliberalism that ravages our continent today—believe another humane and equitable world is possible and are actively looking for ways to build it.

After reading some of Chávez's previous interviews, I realized that he had already discussed several of the topics in which I was interested. It didn't make sense for him to repeat what he had already said to others. Two things, however, helped me decide to go ahead with the project. First, I became convinced that it was possible to further develop several topics already discussed in previous interviews and to add some new ones. And second, the possibility arose to widely disseminate the interview among those who follow my work.

For the sake of time and to offer the reader the maximum information on each topic, I thought it best to introduce my questions with a commentary that synthesizes the main ideas Chávez has addressed in the past in other interviews and speeches—thus allowing me to devote the time available for further exploration as well as to discuss new topics. I drafted a twelve-page questionnaire that—as it turned out, given Chávez's many responsibilities, he never read.

I did not carry out the interview the way I had planned. President Chávez is a great talker, and it was very difficult to get him to focus exactly on the topic of my questions. He usually accompanies his remarks with anecdotes and historical references. In many cases, it seemed he sometimes lost track of the original question or did not want to answer directly, but after a while, and without my insistence, he systematically returned to my question. In other cases, I could not prevent him from repeating the information he had given in other interviews, but this ultimately turned out to be a positive thing because he went even deeper, motivated perhaps by the profile of the reader at which he knew this book was aimed.

I was extremely anxious as I went to my first interview: Would I have what it takes? Would my interviewee understand the crudeness of some questions? Would the tape recorder work? After meeting him and talking to him for a few minutes, all my concerns vanished. I found a down-to-earth, kind, self-critical, reflective man, with a great capacity to listen attentively to my remarks. He was passionate, with great inner strength. I particularly noticed his great human sensibility and his gregariousness. He adores his daughters and sons, and is very tender with them. He cannot live without direct and frequent contact with the humblest sectors of the population, where he knows his greatest strength lies. He knows his people adore him, but he wants to transform that love into organization and autonomous development. He is an extraordinarily human leader—which means that, despite all these virtues, he is not without defects. He himself recognizes that he has a hard time working in a team, loses his patience easily, offends his collaborators, places too much trust in people whom he should not, is unable to organize his schedule in a rational way, and says more than he should: he says the whole truth when he could say part of it.

He does not define himself as a Marxist, but rather as revolutionary and Bolívarian. He is convinced that only a revolution—that is, a profound socioeconomic transformation—can bring Venezuela out of the crisis it has been suffering for decades, and on this topic he is not willing to negotiate, no matter what the cost. He knows that in the Bolívarian revolutionary process the hope of his people, and of many other people of Latin America and the rest of the world, are at stake. He has chosen peaceful means to achieve this revolution and he sincerely believes this is the best way. He has great faith in the role that the people can play as a constituent power to prevent their opponents from obstructing this revolutionary path. "The marvel of our new constitution," he has the habit of saying, "is that it doesn't allow constituent power to be alienated."

Chávez doesn't think he has clear and precise solutions for all the problems that trouble the global Left. He recognizes he doesn't have all the answers, but he is convinced that some basic values should guide him and that he will develop many of his other positions along the way.

Chávez is absolutely clear that there cannot be a revolutionary process without an organized and conscious people. For that reason, he devotes a significant portion of his time to educating the people through his speeches and his weekly radio and television program *Aló presidente*. Obviously, he also places a great value in his direct contact with the people. He tirelessly calls on them to play an active part in the construction of a new society.

Chávez's main focus has been to transform the river of people that protested in the streets on April 12, 13, and 14, 2002, into an organized force. He doesn't miss an occasion to call for the creation of Bolívarian circles of all kinds. He knows that a people who are organized and not disarmed, because they have the support of the army, are invincible. Returning to the interview, in spite of recording more than fifteen hours during June and July of 2002 in various work sessions, in different places throughout Venezuela—a jeep en route to El Vigía, in Mérida; a helicopter to a banana plantation in the same state, from where the program *Aló, presidente* was to be broadcast; the presidential airplane on a return flight to Caracas; La Casona, the presidential residence in Caracas; the presidential residence on Orchid Island, where he was held prisoner in the last hours of the April military coup; the Miraflores Palace, and Fort Tiuna—it was impossible to completely go through the extremely broad questionnaire I had prepared. The biggest gaps were in two areas: the theoretical elements that are the foundation of his project and the political tools he needs to face the enormous challenges. These are topics that he recognizes as still being open.

I found the best way to bridge these gaps temporarily—since I haven't given up the idea of addressing these topics in a more in-depth manner in a future interview—was to supplement with commentary I gleaned from other interviews and speeches Chávez has given. This information appears between or at the beginning of some questions.

These interviews, planned before the April 11, 2002, coup, took place two months later. The information about and analysis of how a ruler deposed by a military coup recovers his post in less than forty-eight hours, a unique event in world history, play an important role in this book.

I would like to finish this introduction with Chávez's final words in the book: "When I reflect on the April 11 coup I remember former U.S. president John Kennedy's ideas, when he said: *Those who make peaceful revolution impossible will make violent revolution inevitable.* We chose to make a constitutional revolution, through a constituent and unquestionably legitimate process. If at any time on April 11 and 12 I doubted that a democratic and peaceful revolution was possible, what happened on April 13 and 14—

when huge numbers of people came down to the streets, to surround Miraflores and several garrisons, demanding my return—vigorously reaffirmed in my mind the idea that this is possible. Of course, the battle is hard, and it will continue to be so. This is the art of making possible what has seemed and continues to seem impossible to so many."

Marta Harnecker

Chronology

NOVEMBER 24, 1948—Overthrow of Rómulo Gallego from the *Acción Democrática* party (AD), leading to dictatorship of Marcos Pérez Jiménes.

JANUARY 23, 1958—Pérez Jiménez's dictatorship falls as a result of a military uprising supported by the *Junta Patriótica Nacional* led by Fabricio Ojeda and whose members include representatives of the then clandestine Venezuelan political parties AD, *Comite de Organización Politica Electoral Independiente* (COPEI), and the Venezuelan Communist party (PCV). The PCV was the most active in the popular uprising that overthrew the dictatorship.

OCTOBER 31, 1958—The Punto Fijo Pact is signed by Rómulo Gallegos, Rómulo Betancourt, Rafael Caldera, and Jovito Villalba. This pact controlled the Venezuelan political system and provides for the AD and COPEI parties to share power. The URD also participated in the meeting but without any significant results for the party. As a result of their participation a group led by Luis Miquilena and José Vicente Rangel split off.

DECEMBER 1958—Democratic elections result in Rómulo Betancourt becoming president.

MAY 4, 1959—The Carúpano and Puerto Cabello rebellion includes civilian and military members of the opposition. Admiral Pedro Medina Silva, the first public leader of the Armed Force for National Liberation–National Liberation Force (FALN–FLN), leads the uprising.

1959–62—The rise of the guerrilla movement FALN–FLN and its adoption of armed struggle influenced by the PCV. Weaknesses under the leadership of Douglas Bravo lead to splits. Guerrilla leaders under Teodoro Petkoff form the Movement toward Socialism (MAS), as a rejection of the traditional parties, the Communist party, and armed struggle.

DECEMBER 17, 1982—The Bolivarian Revolutionary Movement 200 (MBR 200) is born. Underneath the *Samán de Güere* four captains (Felipe Acosta Carlos, Jesús Urdaneta Hernández, Rafael Baduel, and Hugo Chávez Frías) swear an oath.

FEBRUARY 2, 1989—Carlos Andrés Pérez takes office as president.

FEBRUARY 16, 1989—IMF structural adjustment program implemented.

1989—Neoliberal economic reforms: floating interest rates; increased taxes on public services; public salaries increase 5 percent; the progressive elimination of import tariffs; 4 percent reduction in the budget deficit; labor weakened to make work force more flexible. Executive decree allows foreign companies to remit 100 percent of their profits to their base country. Inflation reaches 80.7 percent, real salaries decrease by 40 percent, unemployment reaches 14.0 percent and 80.42 percent of the country is living in poverty.

FEBRUARY 27–28, 1989—*El caracazo*, the popular explosion in response to an increase in gas prices, is put down by the army. An estimated 5,000 people are killed according to human rights organizations. Militarization of life across the country. Curfews imposed on several cities.

DECEMBER 4, 1989—Direct elections of governors, mayors, and representatives with a 60 percent abstention rate. The richest states elect leftist or independent candidates. Militants from the Causa R party were elected to key posts: Andrés Velásquez as governor of the state of Bolívar and Clemente Scotto as mayor of Caroní.

JANUARY 1992—National teachers' strike.

FEBRUARY 4, 1992—Military rebellion led by Lieutenant Colonel Hugo Chávez. Chávez took the San Carlos military barracks in Caracas but failed to take the Miraflores Palace and President Carlos Andrés Pérez gets away. Meanwhile rebels take Maracaibo (where Francisco Arias Cárdenas was), Valencia and Maracay, key Venezuelan cities. Chávez negotiates a surrender and addresses his companions in arms and the entire country on live TV from the Ministry of Defense. He utters the famous words "I take responsibility" and "for now" which catapult him forward as a national leader.

—The MBR 200 is reborn nine years after its creation.

NOVEMBER 27, 1992—Second uprising led by high-ranking officials from all three branches of the Armed Force. The rebels bomb the Miraflores Palace and the Ministry of the Exterior. Rear Admiral Hernán Grüber Odreman takes responsibility for the act. Generals Francisco Visconti, of the army, and Higinio Castro, of the air force, among others, participate. Freddy Bernal, then chief of the special police force and now mayor of Caracas, joins the movement.

MAY 20, 1993—President Carlos Andrés Pérez is impeached by the Supreme Court after being accused of misuse of public funds.

JUNE 5, 1993—Ramón J. Velásquez leads the transition government. The electoral cycle begins and Chávez and the other military prisoners call for abstention; 52 percent of the electorate abstains and Caldera wins.

NOVEMBER 4, 1993—The candidates for the presidency of the Republic include: Rafael Caldera of the Convergencia party and supported by MAS; Andrés Velásquez of the Causa R party; Eduardo Fernandez of the COPEI party; and Claudio Fermin of the AD party. Chávez calls for abstention.

MARCH 26, 1994—Caldera's government grants clemency to Chávez and the other military rebels who were still in prison.

DECEMBER 1994—Chávez travels to Cuba.

DECEMBER 14, 1994—The government intervenes to save fourteen banks. The Central Bank of Venezuela offers extraordinary auxiliary credits to support the banking system. Many banking institutions fail.

1995—Chávez travels the country with the slogan "Constitutional assembly now!"

1996—MBR 200 carries out a survey to see how people feel about electoral participation and whether Chávez should be a candidate.

FEBRUARY 1997— Causa R is divided—one group supports Andrés Velásquez and the other supports the *Patria para Todos* party under Pablo Medina.

APRIL 19, 1997—MBR 200's national assembly decides to participate in the elections and to create a formal political party.

OCTOBER 21, 1997—The Fifth Republic Movement (MVR) is formed.

DECEMBER 6, 1998—Chávez wins the presidential election with 56 percent of the votes in the first round.

DECEMBER 1998—Price of oil on the world market drops to $7.60 per barrel. The external debt reaches US$23.440 billion.

FEBRUARY 17, 1999—National Electoral Council calls a referendum on whether to hold a constitutional assembly.

APRIL 25, 1999—The vote calls for a constitutional assembly and a transitional period begins. The *Polo Patriótico* alliance is formed as a unified front in the elections of representatives for the constitutional assembly. It is composed of MVR, PCV, PPT, and MAS.

JULY 25, 1999—In elections for the constitutional assembly, the *Polo Patriótico* wins 120 out of 131 seats. After the constitutional assembly is sworn in, Congress is dissolved.

DECEMBER 15, 1999—The new constitution is approved in a national referendum.

JULY 3, 2000—Hugo Chávez decrees an increase in the minimum wage to 144.000 Bolívares.

JULY 30, 2000—In the election of 2000, Chávez is reelected president under the new constitution. In addition, 165 legislators are elected to the National Assembly; 23 governors, mayors, and other public officials are elected.

OCTOBER 30, 2000—The Cuban-Venezuelan convention on oil is signed.

JANUARY 2001—Alí Rodríguez, the minister of energy, becomes secretary general of OPEC.

APRIL 2001—Chávez travels through Russia, Iran, Bangladesh, China, and Malaysia.

—Hugo Chávez participates in the third FTAA summit in Québec, Canada. Brazil and Venezuela oppose formalizing the FTAA in 2003.

JUNE 2001—A coup attempt is detected and prevented.

DECEMBER 17, 2001—Bolívarian Circles are sworn in. Chávez relaunches the MBR 200.

APRIL 11, 2002—Coup led by right-wing political parties, business associations, and some high ranking military and labor officials. Pedro Carmona, president of Fedecámaras, names himself president of Venezuela and dissolves all of the branches of government. The coup plotters attack leaders of pro-Chávez groups. Pro-coup gangs attack the Cuban embassy in Caracas.

APRIL 12, 2002—Isaías Rodríguez, the attorney general of the Republic, announces on live TV that Chávez did not resign. Popular sectors and troops loyal to Chávez begin to mobilize against the coup.

APRIL 13, 2002—The popular mobilization against the coup continues to grow. Various groups within the military declare their allegiance to Chávez. In Maracay General Baduel, in charge of the parachute battalion, decries the coup. The people in the streets surround his barracks. In Caracas, the people surround Fort Tiuna and General García Carneiro joins them and puts his battalion in the service of the Chávez loyalists.

APRIL 14, 2002—In the early morning hours Hugo Chávez returns to his post as president of Venezuela. Six officials of the Armed Force and Pedro Carmona are arrested in connection with the coup. Carmona is released to house arrest and a few weeks later he flees to Colombia where he is granted asylum.

AUGUST 16, 2002—In the Caracas district of El Valle there is a massive protest against the Supreme Court's decision that found there had been no coup.

SEPTEMBER 11, 2002—Major protests against Chávez shut down several parts of Caracas.

OCTOBER 22, 2002— Protest in the Plaza Altamira begun by fourteen military officers who come out against the government and are joined by more than eighty other officers. Hundreds of people form a solidarity network to support these officers.

NOVEMBER 11, 2002— PDVSA workers in opposition to the government protest the politicization of the national oil company. Fedecámaras, the CTV and the dissident officers form the "National Reconstruction Pact" to "recover the liberty of the country" and to force Chávez to agree to a recall referendum.

DECEMBER 5, 2002—Campaign to sabotage the oil industry begins. PDVSA's production decreases by one million barrels per day. The Paraguaná refinery, which accounts for 72 percent of the national production, supports the strike. The El Palito and the Puerto La Cruz refineries continue operating but at 50 percent capacity.

DECEMBER 6, 2002—Massacre in the Plaza Francia in the Altamira sector of Caracas: three killed twenty-eight wounded. Not clear who was responsible. Gas, becomes scarce all over the country. Domestic sales of gas are stopped. Forty wells close for twenty-four hours in the north of the Orinoco valley and in Punta de Mata in the southwest part of Maturin.

DECEMBER 7, 2002—*Chávistas* organize a massive march for peace democracy and in support of the constitution.

DECEMBER 9, 2002—Chávez decrees the militarization of the petroleum industry and orders members of the Armed Force to not only provide security but also to operate the industry.

DECEMBER 19, 2002—The Supreme Court declares the PDVSA workers' strike illegal.

DECEMBER 20, 2002—Massive opposition march in Caracas demanding Chávez's resignation.

DECEMBER 2002—Government supporters organize a rally at the PDVSA headquarters. The government retakes the *Pilin Leon* ship with 44 million liters of gas from strikers. Gas production is suspended. The opposition rejects the government's proposal to end the strike. The navy takes control of the *Morwy* oil tanker. The president of PDVSA, Alí Rodríguez Araque, recognizes the collapse of the national petroleum industry. Hundreds of thousands of members of the opposition organize a protest to demand Chávez's resignation.

JANUARY 23, 2003—Hundreds of thousands of people gather on Bolívar Avenue in Caracas to support the government.

FEBRUARY 9, 2003—Chávez announces that the oil coup has been defeated and the country is on the way back to normal production.

MARCH 6, 2003—Chávez appoints a new board of directors to PDVSA with Alí Rodríguez Araque as president.

APRIL 21, 2003—Mission Barrio Adentro health program begins.

JUNE 20, 2003—Mission Robinson, the national literacy plan, begins.

AUGUST 23, 2003—Hundreds of thousands of Venezuelans gather on Bolívar Avenue in Caracas to celebrate the third anniversary of the Bolívarian government.

FEBRUARY 27, 2004—G-15 summit is held in Caracas in the midst of protests with tear gas. The opposition protest results in two deaths and twenty-one wounded. Opposition protestors attack the headquarters of the MVR and the Comando Ayacucho.

FEBRUARY 29, 2004—Massive march in support of Chávez.

JUNE 3, 2004—The CNE announces that the opposition has enough signatures to initiate a recall referendum. Militant *Chávistas* who are convinced there was fraud involved in activating the referendum begin a series of spontaneous, violent protests in Caracas. Chávez accepts the CNE's decision and calls on his supporters to begin mobilizing for the referendum.

AUGUST 15, 2004—The *no* vote (not to recall Chávez) wins the recall referendum by a margin of roughly two million votes.

OCTOBER 31, 2004—Mayoral and gubernatorial elections across the country. Chávez supporters win the vast majority of offices.

JANUARY 19, 2005—The government expropriates the Venepal paper factory and hands it over to the workers for co-management.

JANUARY 30, 2005—President Chávez gives a speech at the World Social Forum in Porto Alegre, Brazil, in front of a standing room only crowd both inside and outside of the Gigantinho stadium.

MARCH 2, 2005—Presidents of Venezuela and Paraguay sign the Caracas Accords.

MAY 1, 2005—Chávez receives a massive workers march in support of the revolution at Miraflores Palace. The opposition workers in the CTV organize a small countermarch.

CHAPTER ONE

Roots

To start the conversation, it would be good to know what factors in your life inspired you politically and what is your vision for the Venezuelan Left?

I entered the military academy in 1970, when I was barely seventeen years old, almost a child. I didn't have any political aspirations: at that time my dream was to be a baseball player. We were a generation of kids from the towns, the neighborhoods, the countryside, who came of age at a time when the guerrilla wars were ending and the country seemed to be beginning a relatively stable democratic period.

I entered the military academy in fairly unique circumstances. I am a member of the first class of what is known as the Andrés Bello Plan. At that time the old military school changed to a sort of military university. Previously, students in the academy earned military bachelor's degrees. My class, however, entered with bachelor's degrees and graduated with degrees in military sciences, which was a university level degree. The curriculum was improved to meet university level requirements. We studied political science and I began to take an interest in military theory. I liked Mao's writings a lot and so I began to read more of his work.

Didn't your brother have an influence as well?[1]

No, because as a young adult I saw very little of my brother except indirectly. He was studying in Mérida and I didn't know that he was involved with the Venezuelan Revolutionary party (PRV-Ruptura) and with Douglas Bravo.[1]

From my readings of Mao I came to several formative conclusions. One of them was that war has a series of variables, or components, that have to be calculated. The Chinese talk about calculating everything, they have a very grounded outlook, they try to stay connected to reality. Mao said that one of these factors was morale, and he suggested that what determined the result of a war was not the machine, the rifle, the plane, or the tank, but rather man, the human being who controls the machine, and, above all, the morale of the man who controls the machine. And secondly, something that I believe is much more important, much broader and more profound: "The people are to the army as the water is to the fish." I always agreed with that and have tried to practice it. I mean, I always had a civilian-military vision. I saw the need for a strong relationship between the people and the army.

During that period I read a lot. I read any book I could get my hands on that dealt with the relationship between the military and the people. Among the readings I did, I remember a book by Claus Héller called *The Army as an Agent of Social Change* (*El ejército como agente de cambio social*). He compiled a series of articles about cases in which the army acted as a social force.

I also read a lot about military strategy, the history of war, Clausewitz, Bolívar, the military writing of Páez, Napoleon, and Aníbal.

We had a very good professor of military history and philosophy—Jacinto Pérez Arcay, who had a military doctorate in history and was a very deep thinker.

Among all these authors you have said that you also studied Marx, although you admit only superficially and that, for this very reason, you can't consider yourself a Marxist, although you also say that you are not anti-Marxist. You maintain that in our countries, since it is difficult to find the working class as defined by Marx in his work, we must go beyond Marxism to discover the solutions to our problems. You aren't a communist but you also aren't anti-communist and you don't have a

problem saying that you have good friends who are communists. Furthermore, you reject a stance that demonizes Marxism or communism.[2]
I also know that you thoroughly studied constitutional law (because it was one of the courses that was required for a degree in military sciences), that they prepared your class to defend the democratic system and that you studied democracy as an institution. You talk about the book Venezuela: A Sick Democracy (Venezuela: Una democracia enferma) *written by a member of the Democratic Action party, that had very interesting ideas.*[3] *You refer to how they defined democracy as a government of the people and, therefore, they focused on who the people are, human rights, and the rights of the people. You also refer to how Bolívar identified democracy with producing the greatest happiness of the people. You have said that you then began to study Bolívarian tracts, and that in the academy you formed Bolívarian societies. On the other hand, you indicate that your generation did not develop, like previous generations, in the School of the Americas.*[4] *Rather, your school was in the Venezuelan mountains and in books about your country. It seems to me that all this information about the development of your generation of the military is extremely important in understanding the Venezuelan military.*

Of course, Marta, another thing that I think influenced me was studying military leadership skills, that is to say, how to direct groups of human beings. One learns how to lift their self-esteem, their morale. I even remember the leadership matrix because for many years I was also an instructor.

Leadership within the Armed Force[5]*?*

No, not only that. I always thought about both aspects: within and without. We are all human beings; the only thing is that one group has a uniform and a rifle and the other doesn't. The soldiers are farmers, boys from the neighborhoods. How does one raise the self-esteem of a group of soldiers out there, on the frontier, people who sometimes don't have enough to eat and are far from their families, without adequate clothing? How does one maintain unity and high morale and self-esteem? How does one inspire nationalism, patriotism, and an understanding of why they are soldiers? How do you talk to them one by one at night, in the morning? How do you attend to their problems? You ask, "Why did you return late from your leave?" "Well, the thing is my mom is sick," "My girlfriend dumped me," "I had a few drinks and I fell asleep." "Well, OK, but try not to do it again, because it is wrong...." Not all members of the military are so worried about their peers, but you do see it a lot.

I know that in 1980, just a few years after graduating, you went back to the academy as an instructor, together with a group of colleagues who had similar interests. And once there you began to recruit for the movement you were organizing at the time.[6] Almost all the rebel officers who participated in the rebellion of 1992 were the best students of that class [1980–1983].[7]

Yes, Marta, during most of the eighties we were working in the military Academy and in the barracks, developing that generation, those Bolívarian nuclei.

Returning to what you said about the army as an agent of social change, I would like to know if the military governments that existed in much of Latin America at the time influenced you.

Of course, the Panamanian as much as the Peruvian. Look, a son of the then-president of Panama, Omar Torrijos, came to our military academy because Panama didn't have a military school. The guy played baseball and so we became friends. And once in a while, I asked him to bring a few of his father's books. I saw photos of Torrijos with the farmers, he told me about the defense force and what he had experienced as a child with his father among the farmers. He told me about the coup d'état that overthrew Torrijos while he was in Costa Rica and how he had to return by passing through the Chiriquí mountains. I became a *Torrijista*. I had several Panamanian friends. That was between 1971 and 1973.

Another thing that influenced me was the coup against Allende.

Let me tell you something: when they overthrew Allende, I was beginning my third year of the academy. In August, the new class that hoped to become cadets had entered and we were in the midst of intensive drills, teaching them to shoot, to stand up straight, the laws and codes of the military, all that; a time of very hard training. One of the new members of a platoon I was training was a seventeen-year-old boy, José Vicente Rangel Ávalos—today the mayor of Sucre—the son of José Vicente Rangel, the current vice president, who was at that time the presidential candidate for the left-wing coalition of parties including the MAS, MIR, the PCV, and so on. Some officials in the academy were of the opinion that this guy should not be a member of the military because he was the son of a communist—remember at that time there were still guerrillas in Venezuela and so they began to pressure me at first to watch this new recruit. "Careful!" they told me, "he is a communist." Later they pressured me to give him bad reports, to look for excuses to keep him down. I chose not to do it. He was a good guy, and besides he was a good student, he had good spirit, and he was a very good shot. Once when he won a shooting prize, an official said to me: "You realize that guy is a guerrilla, he is training." That was [at the same time] they overthrew Allende and because I was already sympathetic with the left-wing movements, that coup affected me. I remember at that moment I thought: "Well, if José Vicente Rangel wins the election, will they order us to overthrow him because he is from the Left?"

The trip I took to Peru in 1974, when I was still a cadet, also influenced me. I was selected to go to Ayacucho for the 160th anniversary of the battle of Ayacucho. I was twenty-one years old, in my last year at the academy, and I had developed clear political aspirations. It was an emotional experience for me, as a soldier, reliving the Peruvian national revolution. I personally knew Juan Velasco Alvarado. One night in the palace, he received me and the other members of the Venezuelan military delegation, and he presented us with a little book, the same size as our constitution [he takes the book version of the constitution out of his pocket and shows it to me]. I saved it all this time, until the rebellion on February 4, 1992, when they took everything from me. The revolutionary manifesto, all my literature, "The Plan Inca," I read them all during those years. And on that trip, between the women, the parties, the parade in Ayacucho, I talked about everything with the young members of the Peruvian military.

All these things were impacting me in one way or another: Torrijos, I became a *torrijista*; Velasco, I became a *velasquista*. And with Pinochet, I became an *anti-pinochetista*.

During that period, I was asking myself: Why the military? To keep them closed up in the barracks? To serve what kind of government? To establish a dictator like Pinochet, or to govern like Velasco or Torrijos together with the people, even challenging the global tendency toward hegemony? So I began to see the military, not in terms of massacring the people, nor in terms of performing coups d'état, but rather as a social service with the Armed Force as a social force.

When I graduated in 1975 I was energized; I already had political ideas, and that was something that had emerged in the academy.

I remember reading that in 1975 they sent you to Barinas, in the Marqueseña, the land of your great-grandfather, and selected you as the communications official for the "Manuel Cedeño" Battalion—in the sixties it was one of the three battalions that had led the army's anti-guerrilla campaign. While you were there, you had lots of time to read because by 1975 there were no longer guerrillas in that area. You said that there—at twenty-one years old—you found a bunch of books, mostly Marxist, in the trunk of decommissioned guerrilla's car, and that you used them to create a library. There was one book in particular that caught your attention: Times of Ezequiel Zamora (Tiempos de Ezequiel Zamora) by Federico Brito Figueroa.[8] You also say that from your readings and experiences during that era, you began to associate guerrillas with hunger and misery; the military chiefs with the government; and the soldiers with the people. You began to reflect on what led people to become guerrillas and so you started over, reading Che and Mao on the topic, searching for the causes, the roots of the revolutionary process. What do you consider your most significant experiences from that period?

There was something that affected me then: I was in an anti-guerrilla theater of operations and one day an intelligence unit brought in some captured farmers and began to torture them that night. I refused to accept that and we had a difficult confrontation. My attitude, refusing to let them torture those farmers, earned me the threat of a court martial for "instigating a military uprising and for failing to recognize authority." That really affected me and I said to myself: "Well, what kind of an army is this that tortures these men? Even if they had been guerrillas there was no reason to torture them."

But I also saw how a group of guerrillas, the Bandera Roja, had massacred soldiers. The soldiers came down, mounted on a truck, half asleep, tired from hiking through the mountains, and the guerrillas were waiting for them in the road. They shot them; they didn't even give the soldiers time to defend themselves and the guerrillas just finished them off. I said to myself: "I am neither in favor of torturing these farmers because they might be guerrillas nor of the guerrillas massacring those soldiers who were innocent guys just doing their jobs." Moreover, this was a guerrilla that had already been defeated, that no longer had any kind of popular support; these were small isolated groups.

When I was fifteen years old, in my native land of Barinas, I knew intellectuals like Ruiz Guevara, an old communist historian who became a good friend; I knew his kids, they were from the Causa R,[9] a political group that had just been formed. Through them I came into contact with the brothers Vladimir and Federico Ruiz Tirado. Vladimir is now a member of the PPT and works with María Cristina Iglesias.[10] He got involved with the Causa R when he was still young and served as a bit of a political mentor for me; he was four years older than me, very mature, very studious; we called him "Popeye." Political discussions and readings dominated that period.

The Ruiz brothers introduced me to Alfredo Maneiro[11] and to Pablo Medina.[12] I spoke with Maneiro in an apartment where I was living in Maracay. It was 1978 and I was twenty-five years old. That was the only time I saw him in my entire life.

I remember Maneiro quite clearly. He said: "Chávez, we have the fourth leg for the table." He was talking about the working class—the leg in Guyana—the unemployed poor, the intellectuals and the middle class, and the Armed Force, which was the fourth leg. And he added: "I am only going to ask one thing of you: You have to agree that whatever we may do, it is not for right now, it is for the medium term, ten years from now." By the way, I remember his theory from that time, that in politics you had to have two things, efficiency and a revolutionary capacity. But, I see lots of revolutionaries who aren't politically efficient, who don't know how to manage. You give them a government post and they fail miserably. But you also find the other kind of people, those who are very efficient but don't have a revolutionary capacity; they don't understand the project. Maniero also talked about the movement, and, more than anything, he was clear on his ideas for strategy.

I liked going into the poor neighborhoods, to see what was happening there, to try to pass unnoticed. I went to Catia[13] to see what the guys from the Causa R were doing there, what their propaganda was like. I even went so far as to put posters up in the streets with a group of them.

That was when, through my brother Adán, I also met Douglas Bravo. Some groups on the left never accepted our process; they wanted to manipulate us; they thought perhaps the military should be the armed wing of the political movement, and I began having disagreements with Douglas Bravo.

My meeting with Maneiro and, why not come out and say it, my certainty that Douglas Bravo's direction was not the right one, pushed me closer to the Causa R, especially because of its work with the popular movements, which was vital to my still developing vision of the combined civilian-military struggle. I was very clear on the idea of the role of the masses, which Douglas's group was not; on the other hand, in the Causa R I felt the presence of the masses.

In another interview, you explained that there were three captains:[14] Jesús Urdaneta Hernández, Felipe Acosta Carlos, and you, who decided to found the December 17, 1982,[15] Movement, although you had already been working on it for three years by then. And Francisco Arias Cárdenas[16] got involved a year later. You founded it two years before the Caracazo,[17] swearing an oath in the Samán de Güere.[18] At that time you called it the Bolívarian Army 200— in honor of Bolívar's two hundredth birthday. You took the "r" off revolutionary because a few officials were suspicious of that term.[19] You describe how the incipient military movement began to form Revolutionary Command Areas (CAR), civilian-military groups in various areas around the country, and surprisingly those groups had indigenous names.[20] You say that every weekend you got together, so you could each discuss the problems in your area, with slides and presentations; that you studied the work of Bolívar, Rodríguez,[21] and Zamora,[22] the tree with three roots that you talk about. According to you, it was after the Caracazo, when other forces and some civilians joined the movement, that it took on the name the "Revolutionary Bolivarian Movement 200."[23]

During that time I began to struggle with the terrible divisions of the Venezuelan Left, with all the conflict within the Left. It was so bad that it even pushed me away because I felt like: "Well, if they are fighting amongst themselves, I am in danger, because they could start fighting with me too and then they might betray me." I had to distance myself for the security of the movement.

What were the repercussions of the Caracazo for the MBR 200?

When the people of Caracas came out into the streets en masse on February 27, 1989, to reject the economic package that had been approved by the then-president Carlos Andrés Pérez, and we saw the massacres that took place in response, it made a huge impact on my generation.

A Venezuelan writer once wrote that on that day the Venezuelan people took to the streets and they still haven't left them. The savage repression made the people retreat, but they continued to fight from their houses: actions, writings, murals all over the place;

small gatherings; a few marches. There were students and social activists killed; there was prison and persecution.

When Carlos Andrés Pérez sent the Armed Force into the streets to repress that social uprising and there was a massacre, the members of the MBR 200 realized we had passed the point of no return and we had to take up arms. We could not continue to defend a murderous regime. The massacres were a catalyst for the MBR 200. We began to accelerate our organizing, our search for civilian contacts and popular movements, to think about ideology, and above all, about strategy: how to transcend one situation and find a transition to a better one.

We discussed how to break free from the past, how to move beyond the kind of democracy that only responded to the interests of the oligarchy, how to stop the corruption. We always rejected the idea of a traditional military coup, of a military dictatorship, or a military junta. We were very conscious of what happened in Colombia in 1990–91 when they organized a constitutional assembly. Of course, it was very limited because, in the end, it was subordinated to the interests of the existing power structures. It was those in power who designed the Colombian Constitutional Assembly and pushed it forward; [the assembly] was a prisoner of the existing power structure and therefore it could not possibly transform the country as needed.

That process was the source of inspiration for the Venezuelan movement called the Patriotic Front. It was a group of intellectuals, a few of them were jurists, who published some communiqués in 1990–91 citing the Colombian example and proposing a constitutional assembly.

We began to request materials, to read, to search for a legal-political advisor, and before February 4, we put forward the argument for a constitutional assembly as the only path out of the trap, out of the false democracy that ended up being nothing more than a power-sharing pact between political parties.[24] We had thought about a few initial plans in case the rebellion was successful. We agreed to issue decrees to convene a constitutional assembly, but of course we hadn't thought it out sufficiently. I believe at that time we did not have the strength or the people mobilized to be successful, but in any case we planted a seed and that was when the country began to ask itself, well, what is this idea of constitutional reform? We began to prepare for the rebellion. We contacted a range of groups that made up the Left. Mostly, we worked with the Causa R. We had meetings, political discussions. I remember asking Andrés Velásquez[25] and Pablo Medina to see how many reservists—guys that had been through military training—were working for SIDOR [Orinoco Steel], to make a list and organize units, to be able to fight for their rights, so that when the time came for the rebellion, we would be able to count on those people with military training. I was thinking about the "Battalions of Dignity" that were organized during the last stages of General Noriega's government to defend Panamanian sovereignty.

When Andrés Velásquez was elected governor of the state of Bolívar, on December 6, 1989, I was being held in custody. That morning they had detained me in the Miraflores Palace, where I was working. I had been fingered as a conspirator within the Armed Force and they were looking for a way to cut me out of the picture; they accused me of planning to kill Carlos Andrés Pérez. I remember that in spite of the fact that I was in custody, I was happy because I realized that Andrés Velásquez had won his election, and I said as much to several friends in the military.

But then things took a turn for the worse. After he took office, I sent him lots of messages through Pablo to try and arrange a meeting. I had taken seriously the idea of the civilian-military unity in Guyana, and I went there covertly several times. I even used a wig to disguise myself because I was under tight surveillance. And I began to meet with members of the military there. I told some of them to get in close with the government and I developed a plan to bring them together.

I decided to tell a member of the military, who was part of the movement and was in charge of the military warehouse there, to present himself to the governor and offer him access to the arms. The idea was to establish an understanding with the government of the state of Bolívar to provide them with products at a low cost. His instructions were to try to become friendly with the governor. The guy tried but he couldn't do it. For me, that was a bad sign and I said as much to Pablo on several occasions. I also tried to get in touch with Lucas Matheus.[26] In violation of the security procedures, I went into a hospital looking for Lucas, and I said, "Look, we need to talk to the governor, to have a meeting." And nothing happened. The last time I sent word to him I said, "I want to see him even if it is at the bottom of the Orinoco River. If he doesn't want us to be seen together then we can put on scuba gear and throw ourselves into the water..." Pablo always tried to defend him though.

Next came the events of February 4, 1992, which by now are pretty well known.[27] The popular protest movement was really unleashed when the people realized that a group of the military was with them. At that time the people passed from a stage of simmering under all the repression to one of explosion. I think that that military rebellion was the biggest of its kind in the history of Venezuela.

We couldn't get together with Andrés, but we did meet with most of the staff of the Causa R. We were working together on the popular component and the military component of the rebellion that we were planning. A few days before it all came together, in a meeting of the national directors, they decided to withdraw their support from the rebellion. But the worst thing was they didn't tell us about their decision although we had already committed to action, to plans of combat. We had previously agreed that they would organize their people to go to prearranged points where we were going to distribute weapons, but only Alí Rodríguez[28] was there waiting with a small group, trying in vain to fulfill their responsibilities. But as a party, the Causa R didn't show up. They publicly hung us out to dry. We had asked them for transportation, communications—that was when cell phones were just coming into use—to edit a pamphlet with some ideas about the constitutional assembly. None of that happened. Later, when they told me about the decision they had made, I didn't want to believe it, because I was still new to politics and I was a soldier, and for me, my word was my honor.

Only part of the Causa R betrayed the rebellion, because as I under-
stand it, the others supported it....

Yes, it was only some of them who betrayed us. Then they began
to split. Pablo Medina stayed firm, although he made the mistake
of not communicating the national directors' decision to us.
Of course we understand that it was a tactical decision and party
discipline, so we don't blame him for it. Until the last minute
we thought we could depend on the entire movement, above all
in Caracas, and especially in Catia where they reported having
strong popular support. We had faith that the people would rise
up, but those of us who were active in the military couldn't direct
the people, nor could we get together because we were in hiding.
We were counting on them and other leaders, not only the Causa
R, but also people from the MEP[29] and other political groups.
I also remember that I brought a truck filled with arms from
Maracay to Caracas but no one ever showed up to get the
weapons. We had agreed to arm groups of the popular resistance
but they didn't take the bait, as I understand it, because of their
divisions and internal conflicts.

How many members of the military participated in it?

The qualitative impact was much more important than the quantitative, because if we even mobilized 10 percent of the regulars, that
is, ten battalions, they were important, elite battalions: heavily
armed units, tanks, paratroopers, antitank missile brigades, etc.,
and this really shook up the internal military structure. We went out
with roughly six thousand men; we moved helicopters, tanks, we
took cities, there was combat at Miraflores, at the Casona [the president's house in Caracas], in Valencia, Maracay, and Maracaibo.
There was no popular mobilization. So it was just us rebelling,
without the people, like fish out of water. Mao said, as you know,
"The people are to the army what the water is to the fish." That
was one of the reasons I decided to give up the arms on the morning of the 4th, around nine or ten in the morning.

That experience made me lose my political virginity—if you will excuse the expression—what with politics, and commitments, and broken promises. Perhaps if Maneiro hadn't died, things would have worked out differently.

What information did those members of the military have about what they were participating in? Did they know exactly what they were up against?

I had my battalion, they were twenty officials and more than five hundred soldiers. Of them, only a very small group of the officials knew what we were going to do that night, the troops didn't know anything. I had a dilemma: I had been trained to be a leader and I felt like if I was their leader, then I couldn't take these guys to Caracas and ask them to risk their lives without telling them what it was all about. So first I called together the officials and explained the military operation. And I told them that if any of them were not in agreement, they could give me their pistol and lock themselves in their rooms until I left with the battalion for Caracas and then they would be free to go home or wherever they liked. Before then, however, I could not let them leave. One of them started crying and said to me: "Don't think I am a coward, but it's my wife, my kids…" "It's OK, go home, but you can't leave until after I do." And that is what he did, and afterward he submitted his resignation, he couldn't deal with the pressure, he was the only one who had asked to stay behind. Later I brought the soldiers together and gave them the same pitch.

Of those six thousand men, how many were taken prisoner?

Roughly three hundred; but not long afterward, the ones who weren't deeply involved in the coup attempt were freed.

A lot of people attacked me for having surrendered. For example, Bandera Roja tried to convince a group of captains that they represented the true revolution and that I had backed out. I guess they didn't know that in any military operation you have the right to retreat. Nonetheless, the fact that I had assumed responsibility for the uprising in front of the TV cameras and that I had said I had surrendered "for now" catapulted me....

And it transformed you into the undisputed leader of the whole process.

Certainly some of the people from Bandera Roja infiltrated the middle ranks of the MBR 200, without having discussed it with the leadership of the movement, and that caused quite a bit of damage. Before the February '92 rebellion they tried to launch a movement within ours, and we had to take measures to stop them.

As you know, a few months later [November 27, 1992] there was another military rebellion and even though we didn't direct it, we joined it from prison. It was a movement within the air force, where there was an important section that had not been able to come out on February 4, and it did so then. Several of those officials had to go into exile. For example, more than sixty officials went to Peru, and one of those is now my secretary. She participated in that rebellion and she went into exile for two years with her husband who was also in the air force.

Those two uprisings brought together a certain military force, but they were unable to draw on popular participation. There was support, but the popular movement did not actively participate in supporting the armed struggle.

After that, we gave up on the idea of continuing the armed struggle.

Why?

Well, because the situation at the time was not ripe for another armed movement. The leaders of the MBR 200 were in prison or had been forced to resign. Those that stayed within the Armed Force were beginning to be persecuted or sent off to remote parts of the country. They were all being closely watched. There was really a kind of persecution that made any coordination impossible.

After those two rebellions we didn't have any military capacity to organize or spark a movement from prison. On the other hand, from a psychosocial and sociopolitical perspective—let's put it this way—removing Carlos Andrés Pérez from office was the ruling class's way of trying to get around a major obstacle, and clearly, in effect, it served as a sort of safety valve. So we denounced it from prison.

While in prison we began to develop some organizational plans to help the still-forming massive support movement take shape. We knew that the people had sympathy for us. But there still wasn't a popular organization to channel the support. So that is when we came up with the idea for the Bolívarian committees. The idea was to move forward, creating small groups that identified with our project. They were clandestine groups because at that time we were persecuted when we were open.

After the February 4 rebellion, the MBR 200 changed substantially, because until then we were a small, clandestine military movement, a group of young officers, a few civilians, a few leftist movements that were incorporated into the MBR 200. But after that date, it was an explosion of emotions more than anything else.

Then came the problems with the 1993 elections. Both Caldera[30] and the Causa R tried to capitalize on the February 4 rebellion.

The Causa R started to use our prison as a symbol of the party and they began suggesting that several members of the military, myself included, were on their board of directors, which was definitely not true. They were working the whole situation, thinking about votes, which ultimately created a lot of problems.

They weren't the only ones either. A lot of people say that Caldera and Aristóbulo Istúriz[31] won the February 4 elections thanks to the talks they gave in our support on the day of the coup.[32] They rode the wave of popular sympathy that our acts produced. I don't deny that they also had their own base of support, especially Aristóbulo who always had a big following among the poor, but that day clearly gave his popularity a boost. Caldera was politically dead in the water, and February 4 brought him back.

Then, we realized that there were people from the Causa R using their family members to lobby us in the prisons to accept candidacies for the December 5, 1993, elections. That was when Arias Cárdenas began to show signs of weakness because we had decided not to participate in the current electoral movement.

So we produced a communiqué from the military prisoners. We came up with some money and it was published in a newspaper, I think it was *Ultimas Noticias*. We said that to get involved in an electoral campaign like that one, which had been controlled by the elite, was to make oneself a deliberate accomplice in undermining the aspirations of the people; that, had they accepted the demand to convene a constitutional assembly, we would have participated. At the same time, we made it clear that we didn't want to disqualify anyone who had decided to participate, knowing that in spite of the current differences they might prove to be future allies. And we ended by saying: "The MBR 200 is not going to participate in the elections, but it will always continue to fight for the country," inviting all who consider themselves to be a "patriotic reserve" and a "hope for the liberation of the masses" to join us. I remember that the communiqué ended with a quote from Simón Bolívar: "All of history indicates that gangrenous politicians will not cure themselves with palliatives."

This position began to cause friction and some officers decided to accept the Causa R nominations. When Arias Cárdenas was released from prison he aligned with that group and went on to win the gubernatorial race in Zulia as the Causa R's candidate. Clearly, he made a strange alliance with them and with COPEI, more with COPEI than with Causa R, because as soon as he won the election he turned his back on the latter.

Besides the communiqué where you established your position, I understand that you all had a campaign in favor of abstention. Could you explain what that consisted of?

A few months before those elections, we began campaigning for what we called active abstention: no to the parties, no to the elections, and yes to the proposal for a people's constitutional assembly. With those slogans, we traveled, visiting several regions, which enabled us to consolidate the organization, mobilize the people, and gather signatures in opposition to the elections. All the work organizing for the abstention allowed us to strengthen the organization of the MBR 200, and to increase its range of action. We talked about a variety of topics with the people: the purpose of the abstention, the idea of the constitutional assembly, our critical appreciation of the political system, etc. We organized forums, workshops, and we also got the word out via a few radio and TV interviews. Those were rare of course, as the mainstream media had already cut us off. I believe that in the end we helped increase the abstention rate, which was higher than all the predictions.

Finally Carlos Andrés Pérez goes to prison amidst a corruption scandal, and the system's rhetoric changes to the line about how his arrest proves that the institutions do function properly. They name Dr. Ramón J. Velásquez as a transitional president until the new elections. Then comes the election buildup in 1993.

At that time there weren't the political, social, psychological, or military conditions for another rebellion. Dr. Caldera won the presidency, and we were let out of prison [after 26 months]. A few of us did not leave the army, others of us were forced out, and as soon as we could we began to travel the country. There were some, like Florencio Porras, who did not leave the army.

He was allowed to stay? They weren't automatically expelled?

No, because we negotiated a deal. The military leaders of the movement, myself included, agreed to request discharges, but on the condition that some of them were allowed to stay. It was all part of the negotiations with the Caldera government.

With the idea that they would continue their work there?

Of course, they were to continue working from within. Florencio and I communicated with each other via family: his parents, his wife, may she rest in peace. I remember little slips of paper, a few contacts, friends, I mean there was an internal movement, but it was highly disorganized. When I was traveling and passed through the state of

Táchira, where he worked, the government closed in on him, sent guards to watch him, or invented any excuse to send him to Caracas.

To prevent any contact?

To prevent even the possibility of a coincidental meeting anywhere in the city. They took away his keys to the arms depots, things like that, until one day he said to me, "I can't deal with this, I'm out."

They all had to put up with that kind of mistreatment, disrespect to their dignity as professionals; sometimes the government wouldn't even let these members of the Armed Force carry weapons. Nonetheless, they fulfilled their responsibilities.

Florencio liked politics and we authorized him to study political science at the Merida State University, where he began his career. I remember that he was still active, politicking in the neighborhoods, until he submitted his resignation and left the army with the rank of captain.

From the prison in Yare we had continued to develop and expand upon the idea of the constitutional assembly. And some of the civilian, intellectual, academic sectors continued writing about the issue. The proposal had a momentary surge of popularity, but then Caldera was elected and the idea was pushed aside until later, when we got out of prison. We left prison to travel the country with that proposal, and above all, we left to push that idea, to develop it. We began to study the theoreticians of constitutional power.

I remember Toni Negri, for example, and his studies of constitutional power, and the French theorists of constitutional power. We studied Rousseau and the *Social Contract* in depth. We also started looking for relevant experiences in Latin America. We went to Bogotá, we talked with the three co-presidents of the Colombian Constitutional Assembly: Álvaro Gómez Hurtado [who was assassinated a few years later], Horacio Serpa, and Antonio Navarro Wolf. We brought lots of documents and also learned about the popular initiatives there. Although many of them were not expressed in the assembly itself, there were proposals for participation.

And so we developed the idea as we went, the seed had been sown on February 4. Little by little, we began to get a broader historical perspective and to talk about constitutional process, not just an assembly. One of the most important things we learned about Colombia was that there really wasn't any process there, it was an event that came to be dominated by the current regime, by the existing power structures.

In those first years, 1994–95, we hadn't ruled out the possibility of reverting to the armed struggle, but we wanted to evaluate the possibilities in terms of real force, and we concluded that we didn't have what it would take.

When Caldera was elected president, we got out of prison[33] and during the next two years (1994 and 1995) we traveled through the entire country. I don't think that we skipped a single city, town, encampment, Indian village, or neighborhood. We went from town to town with the flag of the constitutional assembly, building the organization, strengthening it. For example, we set up local and regional coordinators of the MBR 200. We went from being a clandestine military organization to a popular movement, though there was always a military presence; it was a civilian-military movement.

After getting out of prison, we developed our strategic map that began with the MBR 200 and its political allies—we had identified them before making our alliances with them: Causa R and other smaller groups. Then, below, we drew the "independents," who weren't actually independent but were the military sectors that could not be mentioned explicitly. It was 1994 and we were being persecuted, so the MBR 200 was still semi-clandestine.

Social and political groups were key to navigating our way; so we recognized the need to establish alliances. Then we brought together several projects, one of which was the popular constitutional assembly; others included defending people's standard of living, defending national sovereignty, and the power polynomial. Those projects were included in a mega-project called the "organization of the popular movement." Here on the map we had a long-term transitional program on the national level. Down below we had Latin America and the Caribbean, and, further down, other global allies. We developed the map over the course of years. Giordani[34] did an amazing job with this project; the engineer Héctor Navarro,[35] Ciavaldini, and others contributed as well.

Then, in the mega-project we called the organization of the popular movement, we began filling in the content of each project: each one needed a motor to drive it forward. We began to have formative experiences, even back then. That is where we got the idea for the Bolivarian committees of the constitutional assembly. The idea was that they were to be instruments for organizing the popular movement. The project in defense of people's standard of living did not advance very far, although it did create a few groups to combat unemployment, groups to defend citizen security, and groups to fight against the price increases. National sovereignty meant thinking about our borders, and the polynomial of power included the church, the Armed Force, the business community, to try to bring together powerful players beyond the social groups that we were allied with.

I wanted to talk to you about this so that you understand that we had studied our strategy. And the need to make contacts with the Venezuelan Left was always part of the strategy, but in practice we made very little progress gaining support because of people's lack of faith, justified, perhaps, by the rest of Latin America's political experiences. I still use this strategic map, though now it has been revised and updated.

Once we analyzed the situation, we realized that another military insurrection would have been crazy. From the military point of view, our movement was primarily led by former members of the military—who enjoyed wide support and had generated high expectations among the people—but the movement within the military was severely weakened and reduced, with little capacity to organize another military uprising because the majority of its leaders had already been detected. I should add that the government had taken internal measures to prevent another insurrection—strengthening their units, sending people to key sites, etc.

From the social perspective, we dedicated ourselves to finding out what the people thought. And, if indeed there have always been some popular currents supporting armed struggle, on those trips across the country we realized that a large share of the population did not want a violent movement, but, rather, they expected that we would organize a political movement structured to take the country on the right path.

Although all our information suggested this was the popular opinion, we still wondered if we should continue to support active abstention, and hold off entering electoral politics until later, or if we should wait until we had better mobilized the various forces that gave us our strength so as to proceed via a strategy not involving elections, or, alternatively, if we should move forward with the elections immediately.

So we decided to consult the people through a poll, though it ended up being much more than a poll. We organized teams of psychologists, sociologists, professors, and also students; we also sought to integrate people who were not from the movement in order to maintain objectivity.

We surveyed one hundred thousand people between 1996 and 1997. I remember that we divided the country into east, west, and middle, and everyone in the movement helped conduct the survey. The survey had two main questions designed for quantitative analysis. The first, "Do you support Hugo Chávez's candidacy for president?" and the second, "Would you vote for him?" The results of this process gave us the green light to move forward. I remember that the responses to the first question tallied up to around 70 percent yes and 30 percent no. That result was totally clear: the people wanted me to run for president. The second question, would you vote for Chávez, returned a positive response in 57 percent of the surveys, and surprisingly that was exactly the same percentage of the votes I won in the election two years later.

I remember that Giordani, Navarro, also a university professor of planning and mathematics, Nelson Merentes,[36] a mathematician, and I began to play out the possibilities on a computer. We even incorporated those computer generated scenarios into our strategic planning.

We thoroughly debated what direction to take. At that time, there were plenty of contradictions; some groups were against the electoral route, and they left the movement. They accused us of having abandoned the revolution because we had discontinued the armed struggle, but who ever said that arms guarantee a revolutionary orientation? As often as not, weapons have been at the service of the counterrevolution. There are still some individuals or groups that are critical of the electoral process, but others have come back.

We knew taking the electoral path was a strategic decision that could be catastrophic, that we could walk right into the trap that the system set for us, that it could lead us into a pit of quicksand.

Finally we made the strategic decision to move forward peacefully, but when I talk about this decision—as you know—I always point out that our movement is peaceful but not disarmed, we have weapons to defend it. I think that became clear when the oligarchy and a large part of the military elite caused that hullabaloo back on April 11 [2002].

I remember when we were in the process of choosing the electoral strategy; we always talked about the "strategic window." For us, the elections were our strategic window, and we always knew, as the computers indicated when we did the calculations, that our strategic window could bring us to the brink of horrible possibilities, that we ran the risk of falling into the system's web. When we chose the electoral route, we did so fully aware that we ran that risk, Marta. I was deeply afraid that I would end up negotiating, compromising.

Until 1996 we had chosen not to participate in the elections. Really, we were calling for abstention as the tactical element in a strategy to force a constitutional assembly, which was always our plan.

So that is how we chose to go down this road. Now, you are probably wondering, why do you insist so strongly on that road? I will tell you: because we believe in it, not only as a tactic, but also because we believe that strategically it is possible, we said it millions of times, "we are going to win the presidency of the Republic to bring the power to the people, to organize a constitutional assembly." I myself had many doubts about the possibility of breaking through the system's barriers point-blank and transitioning to a different status quo, but we did it. That same year, 1999, we held the referendum.

CHAPTER TWO

A Peaceful Transition; A Painful Institutional Birth

You have said from the very beginning the MBR 200 rejected the idea of a traditional military coup, of a military dictator or junta, and that even before the February '92 rebellion you had put forward the idea of convening a constitutional assembly. The idea, according to what you have said, was to find a way, whether through armed struggle or through a peaceful electoral process, to allow the country to break with the past in order to accomplish the national transition that it so needed. Could you explain how it was that that idea developed?

Here in Venezuela almost nobody was talking about a constitutional assembly. A lot of people didn't even know what that was. We designed a methodology to explain the constitutional process so that our people didn't limit themselves to seeing the constitutional assembly as the goal, as the end. We divided the process into stages.

We identified the first stage as the awakening of constitutional power: the transformation of strength into real potential. I remember that I used the example of ice that melts and flows as water, or a rock that is on top of a mountain and falls, unleashing an avalanche, something along those lines. And from our point of view, that occurred on February 27, 1989, with the *Caracazo*.

The events of February 4, 1992, came next. The popular protest was unleashed when the people realized that a sector of the military was supporting them. In that moment, as I have told you, the people went from a stage of repressed boiling to one of explosive expansion.

So the challenge at that time was how to convene a constitutional Assembly through legal means. The first thing we had to do was win the presidency of the Republic in order, from that position of power, to call for a referendum where the people could speak for themselves. We based our position on article 4 of the old constitution, which basically said: "Sovereignty resides with the people who shall exercise it through suffrage (a referendum is a form of suffrage), through the institutions of public power, and so forth." Our juridical interpretation of that article allowed the president to call a referendum so that sovereignty, which resided with the people, could express itself through an institution of public power.

We were able to win the referendum on the constitutional assembly, and although the opposition was on the attack, saying: "with the constitutional assembly we don't eat, we don't build highways, we don't construct houses," the idea stuck at the national level. At that stage, we called it the chapter of convening the constitutional assembly.

The elections for representatives to the constitutional assembly came next. Candidates from the political parties participated in those elections, but so did journalists, indigenous peoples, and singers, some at the national level and some at the regional level. An incredible number of people ran in elections for one of the 130 representatives in the constitutional assembly.

Once the members of the constitutional assembly had been elected, we entered the assembly stage: the assembly deliberated on and framed the new constitution.

I've heard that the idea was to include popular participation in the discussion process for the new constitution, and that there were even people planning how practically to facilitate that popular participation. But then, all of a sudden, it was cut off and the framing of the constitution became a very closed process, which the people did not follow or participate in.

I believe the process of framing the constitution was quite open. I
believe there was a lot of participation, but what happened was that
we had to set a time limit on the process. A large debate would have
interfered with the speed at which the political process needed to
move forward. The constitutional assembly was elected on July 25,
1999. It convened in August and in December it concluded the debate
on the constitution, which was then voted on through a popular referendum. Certainly, there are sectors that would have liked the process
to be slower, more thorough. But, in spite of that, I believe that there
are no precedents in the recent history of this country of so open a
process and of so thorough a debate. How was it done, for example,
with the constitution of 1961? The people elected a congress and that
congress granted itself the power to write a constitution. It was elected
to write laws and, nevertheless, it chose to draft and approve a constitution. That was indeed a constitution framed in a closed format.

There was no referendum?

Here, in all of Venezuelan history, there had never been a referendum. The first was the one that we convoked on February 2, 1999, to
ask the people if they agreed to calling for a constitutional assembly.

Once the constitutional assembly was installed, it wrote its own
regulations and created a participation commission—they called it
something like that—whose task was to encourage participation,
receive diverse proposals, and discuss them and take them to the
assembly.

Toll-free telephone lines were opened, so that people could provide their opinions; the assembly delegates organized regional
assemblies to receive input—at least our delegates, who were in the
majority, did. I believe that once or twice per week they went to the
regions from which they were elected to organize assemblies, to
talk, to explore ideas, to look for projects.

Now, sure, there are some who imagined a more radical, more
participative, constituent process and they thought, as you said,
about the technical mechanisms to do this. That is possible. Some
said that the discussion process should have lasted two years.

Imagine that! That each article should be put to a referendum rather than approving the constitution as a whole. That might well have amounted to nothing, as has happened in other countries.

Sometimes it is necessary to sacrifice some important things for the sake of expediency, and at that time it was urgently necessary to transform the political map, to be able to continue moving the revolutionary project forward. I remember that when I was elected president of the Republic, the AD and COPEI parties continued to dominate the Supreme Court. We were going to encounter a serious obstacle there. We had only three governors who supported our project, the majority were with the same two parties. Also, the National Congress was in their hands—we were the minority. Now, Marta, to be realistic, one must connect ideas with reality—in this case I am referring to the speed of the political process.

Soon we passed into the approval of the constitution phase. Over 70 percent of the voters in the country said yes to the new constitution.

And finally came the longest phase and most complex phase: the executive phase. We took the term from Toni Negri.

In this phase, the first step was to elect the new authorities for transforming—as I told you—the political map of the country. We were able to relegitimize, through new elections, all the powers in the country: presidents, governors, mayors, legislative representatives.

During the process of putting together the candidacies of representatives, governors, and mayors, problems arose due to disputes around positions within the electoral political coalition that we had created. Among others, the coalition included the Patriotic Pole, which united the Fifth Republic Movement (MVR), the party Fatherland for All (PPT), the Venezuelan Communist party (PCV), sectors of the Movement Toward Socialism (MAS), and the People's Electoral Movement (MEP).

I have heard that the MVR was very sectarian and tried to force its candidates into any available political position. I have also been told that at that time you harshly attacked the PPT in public. Is that true?

There is something to all of that, though in absolute terms, no. I cannot deny that at times there was sectarianism in the MVR. Unfortunately these shortcomings are an inherent part of politics. But, if you broadly review the events, you will see that few parties in our coalition of that time have opened as many spaces as we have to candidates from other parties.

So how do you explain the split with the PPT?

The situation with the PPT was a result of the fact that neither we nor they were able to put our joint strategic project before our secondary differences and the regional damage they caused. I remember that the first day of the campaign we had a huge march from downtown Caracas to Petare. Our candidate for mayor of Petare, José Vicente Rangel Ávalos, the current mayor, was there, but since the PPT had another candidate—because we weren't able to come to terms on the issue—they had mounted a sound system up above and were using it to broadcast their slogans in the middle of our rally. When our candidate was talking, they began to interrupt, and I could not contain myself. The rally was being broadcast on national television, but this is how I am, I took the microphone from Pepe Rangel and said: "Are they going to let us proceed with our rally or did our friends from the PPT come to sabotage us?" And Pablo Medina was there and I told him: "Pablo, please, this is a national event, let Rangel talk." I called for order. They were quiet but then they started interrupting again. That was a sectarian attitude, dirty politics, trying to take advantage of our rally to shout their slogans. That was the first confrontation. From that point things only got worse with the gubernatorial candidates.

I've been told that the MVR and the PPT made a deal that the PPT would support your presidential campaign, but they would put forward their own candidates in some local elections, and that as part of the agreement you would not publicly appear in support of MVR candidates when they were being contested by PPT candidates. They say that you did not hold up your end of the agreement.

Marta, I never agreed to that. I tell you, my conscience is clear on this issue because I did everything I could to come to agreement in some of those regions. Later, the PPT sabotaged our rally in Guarico. Our gubernatorial candidate was speaking, and there they were, shouting. The crowds even came to blows. They started a brawl and a lot of people left the rally. So in my talk that day, I really gave it to them. After I gave that talk, they organized a meeting of their national directorate and they decided to split, and they stopped supporting my candidacy.

My harsh words were in response to their undisciplined attitude and sabotage of our events, which was manipulated to look like lack of respect for them on my part. I think that had a strong influence on Pablo, he was always very reticent about that alliance. Pablo was the last one of them to decide to support my candidacy the first time, and after that he kept a low profile, he didn't campaign.

I was always very clear on the importance of the National Assembly as a strategic space to be won. In the first speech I gave after the election campaigns began, I said that I would trade all the mayoralties and governorships for the National Assembly. It was crucial that we win the majority of those seats because the majority was going to determine the composition of the other key government offices: the attorney general of the Republic, the Supreme Court, the electoral branch, the citizen branch.[1] And it was crucial to have good members of the National Assembly in order to produce revolutionary laws, but no, tactical errors weakened our strategy and we are still suffering because of those errors.

The PPT, a very solid party, withdrew from the alliance, went to elections on their own, and did not get a single one of their candidates elected. The MAS occupied the space the PPT vacated. Unfortunately, a good number of the people who joined the National Assembly ended up being of weak political and ideological fiber. Take Puchi or Mujica[2] who are truly willing to compromise on anything. Now we have a National Assembly with severe shortcomings and it is causing problems. The National Assembly should count María Cristina Iglesias, Vladimir Villegas,[3] Aristóbulo Istúriz, José Albornoz[4] among its members. There are some twenty good members of the PPT who ought to have been elected to the National Assembly.

It was impossible to resolve our political differences at the time and so we went to the National Assembly with a very narrow majority. And, in order to get the two-thirds of the assembly required to appoint members of the Supreme Court and the rest of the government positions, we had to compromise all the time—with the AD, COPEI, and the Venezuelan Project. They put forward unqualified candidates for various government positions. That is why in the Supreme Court today you see a group that is not qualified to honorably fulfill their duty and who are manipulated politically because of their historic ties to the AD, to COPEI, or other counterrevolutionary sectors.

Pablo Medina never accepted my leadership and he ended up leaving the PPT and on the day of the coup, he showed up in Miraflores. The day before he had been seen on TV next to Carlos Ortega,[5] lecturing and agitating against Chávez and against the Bolívarian revolution. Fortunately there is a group of fighters like María Cristina, Aristóbulo, and many more who carry the original banner of the Causa R, the same party that Alfredo Maneiro founded.

You have said that one of Pablo Medina's shortcomings is that he would not accept your leadership. Could it not also be that it is hard for you to accept the leadership of others?

In truth, it isn't hard for me.

At any point in your life have you had to recognize the leadership of anyone besides yourself?

Yes, as a prisoner, when we were preparing for the second military rebellion, a different group of military leaders came up. I remember that we sent letters and notes from prison to prepare for the second rebellion that we expected in June or July, mainly with people from the army. Then we received information in prison, via one of the army officials who was still free, that people from the navy and the air force were also preparing another movement. Having received this news, we decided to stop our movement and I was one of the ones who sent word that I recognized the command of those outside the prison. I was one of the ones who said: "We are prisoners, with profound limitations; the leadership is out there: Admiral Grüber, General Visconti, Admiral Cabrera Aguirre, and Colonel Virginio Castro." They formed a military political command. At that time, for example, I recommended that they incorporate Pablo Medina into that political command and they did. The circumstances showed that I could not be the leader.

I believe that was the only time I recognized someone else's leadership, because since then there has not been a similar situation. I am not the leader because Hugo Chávez decided to be the leader. I came out of prison to the street to see what was happening, to travel the country and try and organize the people. In the process of accomplishing those tasks, a natural leadership arose that I cannot capriciously delegate to another person because of pressures or deals. I believe in natural leaders, not in those that are imposed. And if I ever believe that my leadership has weakened so much as to put the process at risk, and another leader arises, I will not have any problem supporting that person, not any problem whatsoever.

I am very much aware of what Bolívar once said: "I am but a light feather dragged along by the revolutionary hurricane." Leaders find themselves in front of an avalanche that drags us forward. It would be very unfortunate, sad, if a revolutionary process of change were to depend on a *caudillo*. The human being is so vulnerable. There are so many reasons: either they are bought or they sell themselves, or they are corrupted, or they get sick, or they infect others…. Look at what happened with the five-year federal war: it basically depended on the fighter Ezequiel Zamora. On January 10, 1860, in San Carlos, one bullet, just one, was enough to kill Zamora, and with him, the hope of a people died. The revolution turned to anarchy, retreated, failed, and the ruling class and the oligarchy held on to power and spread their hegemony over all the mechanisms of power.

Some people point to me as the cause of all society's problems, others as if I am the benefactor, responsible for everything good, but I am neither the former nor the latter. I am but a man in particular circumstances, and the most beautiful part is that an individual human life is capable of contributing to the growth, the awakening of the collective strength. That is what matters!

After Pablo left the PPT we were able to rebuild our alliance. Now I have several members of that party in the government: Aristóbulo Isturiz, María Cristina Iglesias, Alí Rodríguez at the head of the PDVSA [Venezuelan Petroleum Company], Julio Montes as ambassador to Cuba, and many more members who are working in the streets. And I feel like all those tactical differences from before have gradually been forgotten.

This phase in the execution of the constitution is without a doubt the most complicated. It is about legislating and gathering strength so that this constitutional project—the revolutionary constitution—does not get left behind as only theory, on the drawing board, as a utopia, as a dream. We must firmly root it in reality.

The government empowered by the National Assembly wrote, as you know, forty-nine laws. Among them are: the Lands Law, the Bank Law, the Microfinance Law, the Fishing Law, the Hydrocarbon Law, laws that affect the historic interests of the oligarchy, of the ruling classes. When these classes saw that we had decided to deepen the process, and that we were about to transform the socioeconomic structure, they began to work toward their failed April 11 coup.

I want to be clear: I always said that the executive phase should not be characterized—because it would be suicide—by the suspension of constitutional and constituent power and protection. We always felt that the power of the constituents should not be frozen, but rather that it should continue to be active with established power structures and representatives of the people and of the diverse groups in civil society, that we should not commit the mistake of taking power away from the people from whom our power derives.

April 12 and 13 showed that the root power of the people is alive and well. If that power had been frozen, if it had been asleep or if it had been the victim of blackmail or repressive threats, the coup attempt would have succeeded and the existing government powers—representative of the power of the people's participatory constitution—would not have been able to reinstall themselves. That constitutional power did not permit the expropriation of their rights and it firmly demanded their protection with the support of sections of the military.

Was your belief that you cannot achieve a true social transformation without changing the rules of the game, that is, without changing the constitution, influenced to a certain extent by the Chilean experience and the problems that Allende confronted when he attempted to achieve profound social change within the limits of the representative democratic bourgeois system?

I can say that the Chilean experience, the experience of the Popular Unity, did not influence my perspective much, but it did influence Carlos Matus, a Chilean economist who was one of Allende's ministers. He put forward, in one of his books, that if a political force is to be transformative, it should be able to exercise leadership, it should be able to identify the weakest front of its adversary—this is an idea that is clearly applicable to military science—and attack via that front. Society has three kinds of structures: political-legal structures (the recipient), socioeconomic structures (the content), and ideological structures (the context). He argues that whoever tries to transform society must be able—through science and calculation—to determine which of those three structures is the weakest and to attack via that structure. If you are wrong and you attack via your adversary's stronger front, you will fail, tie yourself down, or lose momentum until you cease to be a revolutionary transformative force. We used his methodology to analyze the Venezuelan situation and that is how we decided to begin our attack on the political-legal structure, because it was the weakest of them all, and, as you see, we were not mistaken. I thought our adversary was going to put up even more resistance in 1999, but our attack was rapid and decisive. We struck for the heart, they did not have time to regroup, and here we are today.

Now, these things are never easy. We are in the midst of a difficult battle, because the new must be constructed on the ruins of the old, and that is where the bad habits hold you back. Up until now we have changed the overall political-legal structure, but because of the nature of our peaceful and profoundly democratic process, this structure is still marked by its old vices, infiltrated by adversaries, and sometimes our own ranks are weakened by loss of revolutionary consciousness. This is why we have not been able to eliminate the scourge of corruption.

Some might feel cheated because the result is not what we wanted, but who ever said that a process of this magnitude, with goals of this scale, was going to achieve the ideal political-legal structure in just three years? Now, I am sure that we are on the right path. How many more years will it take? If it is about throwing out a date, I would say that we will reach the end of this process in 2021. Maybe earlier.

I know that in a few places highly unqualified people have been appointed to positions of power and that they have participated in corruption. Who appointed them?

The previous minister of the interior and justice, Luis Miquilena. In spite of the fact that he fulfilled an important responsibility during the constitutional phase, he later lost sight of the project. Friendships, interests, perhaps pressures, maybe his age, I don't know how many factors influenced him. One night, he ended up saying that I had to step back and give in to one of the demands of the opposition by eliminating the Laws of Empowerment *(Leyes Habilitantes)*. I responded: "You know that I will not do that because those are the laws that enable us to enter into a new phase of developing the application of the constitution." He reacted by telling me that we could not make a revolution, that revolutions are either violent or they don't happen, that the most we could do here in Venezuela was to change a few things, make some reforms, but that we had run up against the force of the opposition and that we had to begin to manoeuvre. Can you imagine that the guy who was suggesting this was my own minister of the interior? That was shortly before the December 10, 2001, strike.

While we are talking about Miquilena, there are those who say that he was very influential in determining the current composition of the National Assembly; that he was behind the alliance with MAS...

That's true. He was also influential in the composition of the Supreme Court and the attorney general's office.

Why did you support Miquilena and not someone more solidly from the Left?

To understand my relationship with Miquilena, you have to consider the whole process. At this point we can say plenty of negative things about him, but even though there had been some criticisms about his control of the party and other issues, a year ago none of us could have imagined what was going to happen. It was hard to imagine that a person with such a long history of struggle on the left would end up like he did. There is even a novel called *The Death of Honorio (La Muerte de Honorio)* by Miguel Otero Silva, which refers loosely to his life.

Miquilena started off as a union leader, back in the forties. I think he was in the Communist party and later founded a movement called "Black Communists." That group supported the government of Isaías Medina[6] on October 18, 1945, when members of the AD organized a coup. He was incarcerated in Ciudad Bolívar for seven years during the dictatorship of General Pérez Jiménez; many of the old leaders of the Left met him in that prison. When the Pérez Jiménez government fell, he got out of prison and was very close with Jovito Villalba of the URD; then they founded a party that put José Vicente Rangel forward as a presidential candidate. That is most of what I know about his history; there are, of course, people who know him much better.

Now, how did I meet Miquilena? One night my cell phone rang— I had a cell phone hidden in the prison—and the voice on the other end says to me, "I'm Miquilena." The name sounded familiar but I knew very little about him—everything I just told you about him I learned later. The name was familiar because previously, someone had set up a lawyers' office in Caracas where we had secret meetings, and where I sometimes even slept. I carried the key, opened the office, and waited for the officials. In the office there was large desk with a nameplate that read "Luis Miquilena." That name stuck in my mind. I am talking about a year or two before February 4, 1992, but I never knew who that was, nor did I ask whose office it was. We just used the office for meetings.

When he called me on my cell phone, I made the connection— Luis Miquilena…. "Oh!" I said to him, "the office, and so on and so forth." He said, "That office belonged to one of my brothers, a lawyer, who died. I shared it with him, and lent it to Pablo Medina." It was Pablo who had gotten the keys to the office and given them to me. I remember Pablo told me: "*Comandante,* a group of old friends and I—they were, I believe, throwing back a few drinks in Maracay— want to show you our solidarity; I am going to pass you to doctor so and so…." Later, I talked to Luis again and he told me: "*Comandante,* I have lived a full life and I want you to know something—you are stuck in there, but you invested for the long haul and you are a young man who is going to collect." Then he told me that he wanted to visit me and I included him in my list of visitors. In the prison we were allowed to receive visits only from people on a list that we drew up for the authorities. He visited me like two or three times and got to know the people there, the other comrades in prison. For me this is all still a bit painful, because I had a lot of affection for that man.

Then I got out of prison and the first day, there Luis was, loyally waiting for me. I remember the first thing we did was to go to tape a TV show called *José Vicente Hoy*, with José Vicente Rangel. It was a Friday. Luis was a good friend of José Vicente's going back many years. Then we left for Carlos Fermín's house—another good friend. He was living in a small apartment where I could see the show while we talked and made toasts. I slept in his apartment that night and I have warm memories of him and his wife, Yomaida.

The next day I was in the street, the hurricane carried me. I remember that Miquilena lent us an old Mercedes-Benz that he had and basically never used. We used it to carry some weapons. Once they stopped that damned car with some rifles in it and, well, there was a scandal in the media: "Miquilena's car has been confiscated by the DISIP." The guy who drove the car was arrested and Miquilena was reported to the police because he was the owner.

Since I didn't have anywhere to go, I bounced around from here to there. Luis told me: "Look, Hugo, there is an extra room in my apartment, if you want, feel free to go there." That is how I ended up spending several months living in a small apartment that he has near the Plaza Altamira, in the building called "Universo 6." I spent several Christmases and New Year's Eves there. There was a lot of dialogue, and a lot of people went there....

Luis was one of the people who promoted the pro-constitutional assembly front and began to look for resources, to collect money. He was outside of politics until he joined in that effort. Then we grew apart, the pro-constitutional assembly front did not work, and so I distanced myself with my small group.

Who were the other people I was in contact with? Basically, there were no other relationships. Remember that I was not well liked in many sectors of the Left or at least amongst their leadership. I already told you about the problems that were developing with the Causa R.[7] When they showed up for the elections we were calling for active abstention. I remember our slogan was "For now, for none: constitutional assembly now!" Andrés Velásquez, and Pablo Medina said that by calling for abstention I was interfering with their political development, that I didn't understand politics and so on and so forth. They put forward Arias Cárdenas. He certainly was intelligent, a true leader, but Chávez was crazy. I am talking about the Causa R, the political movement that you could say was closest to us because all the leaders of the MAS were for Caldera.

The Left most loyal to its ideals, including the PCV, had differences with me. I remember, for example, that one time a group of workers invited me to a meeting they had in Central Park in order to prepare for the May 1 march—an alternate march to the one organized by the CTV, with the CUTV and all those leftist movements, the Communist party, and others. OK, so I arrived at the meeting and I sat down in a random chair. All the leaders who were there at the head table saw that I had arrived but didn't greet me. I never forgot that and it is part of the answer to the question you asked me. Imagine, I was trying to present myself to the political Left, I was being watched, persecuted, defamed, et cetera, and the leaders treated me like that.

What year are we talking about?

About 1994 or 1995. Like I was saying, I arrive at their event, I sit down, I was trying to be humble. There were a lot of people there. The room was full. A few people came up from behind to greet me, but I was trying to hear what they were saying from the podium, without interrupting or causing a scene. So, while those at the table were talking, someone in the room let out a shout: "So you guys aren't even going to greet *Comandante* Chávez" and applause followed. Only then did those leaders welcome me.

On the other hand, I knew that in another assembly of those small leftist groups, they had concluded that I was a messianic leader in contradiction with the movement and the interests of the masses. The official bourgeois discourse infected and destroyed the Left. I don't deny my mistakes, I have certainly made some, but those groups rejected and condemned me. That explains why I was involved with some retired military leaders and a few political leaders who were not from political parties, including Luis Miquilena, Manuel Quijada, and others, but not many.

Moreover, I was a leader without resources. Sometimes I didn't even have enough money to buy gas, we hiked from here to there in small groups; many of us were arrested. Once in a while—once or twice a year—José Vicente Rangel invited me onto his TV show; once in a while Alfredo Peña[8] also invited me on his program. I remember I called a press conference because I was coming back from a trip to Cuba, and only two journalists showed up.

Facing this harsh reality, our local leaders in most every state were finding themselves going up against not only the Right but also against the Left. Our movement, MBR 200, cut its teeth in confrontations with MAS, with the Causa R, confrontations with all those groups. I want to be clear: Miquilena was never a leader of the MBR 200. He played a support role, organized meetings, participated in group discussions —he was always for the constitutional process.

Then we decided to participate in the 1998 presidential elections and the Communist party broke the blockade. As soon as we announced our decision to go to the elections, they said, "We support *Comandante* Chávez's candidacy."

Then we began to meet with groups and people, and that was when Miquilena got involved, because he is skilled politically. He organized the meetings with sectors of the Left, because I often did not have the patience to deal with those interminable discussions with the Causa R, with sectors of MAS, and with other smaller parties like the MEP.

So he began dialogue, looking to form alliances, as my spokesperson. That's how we were able to form the *Polo Patriótico* and Miquilena assumed a leadership role, showing great political skill; he earned a lot of respect among allies and potential allies alike.

I remember, for example, the first meeting I had with Fedecámaras, with Francisco Natera. Back then he was the president of that institution. Who was it that organized that private meeting at his house? Luis Miquilena. It was the same deal with meetings with business leaders, Miquilena was almost always involved, lobbying, making contacts. That is how he eventually became our spokesman with politicians, with business interests, and even with the ministers of the Caldera cabinet.

We used Miquilena's house shortly before the elections to meet with Maritza Izaguirre, who was Caldera's minister of finance. Faced with the evidence that I had a good chance of winning, she wanted to meet with me, to explain a few economic issues.

To sum up, and keep my answer from getting any longer, I believe there are many reasons why Luis Miquilena became a spokesman, a director of that campaign. And I believe that in spite of all the errors he made and his quirks he played an important role in building unity for the elections, and in designing our electoral strategy.

And then, when I took office as president, I appointed him minister of the interior—an essentially political ministry, since at that time we did not have a vice-president—precisely because he brought the profile, experience, and political know-how. And then, three months later, I asked him to go work on the constitution because I was too tied down with problems in the government, with the disaster I had inherited, to focus on that issue. And that is how he became practically the director of the campaign for the constitutional assembly, gathering the funds, drawing up lists, etc. He had a huge influence on that project. I believe he played a role, albeit with many errors, not all of which are his responsibility because it would be wrong to blame him for all the problems.

Going back to the issue of old vices, a lot of people are upset because rather than decreasing, corruption seems to have increased: public services charge extra under the table, and there have been no arrests or prosecutions for corruption. How should this be understood within a movement that raised its flag in the name of fighting corruption—a flag that others around Latin America, such as the Workers party in Brazil and the Wide Front in Uruguay, have hailed as allowing the greatest advances on the left?

I recognize that we still have a long way to go on that issue, nothing remarkable has been accomplished in combating corruption, nothing that could be called substantial or defining. But I also don't think things are worse now than they were before. One would have to do a more thorough, objective analysis to ascertain that.

Corruption here, as in much of Latin America, is a cultural phenomenon, an extremely difficult phenomenon to fight against; it is something that occurs not only at high levels but also at the lowest levels. It is like a cancer that has metastasized in all directions. That has to be understood from the beginning.

Compton

Clearly, the political opposition consistently argues that nothing has been done to reduce corruption. I think that a lot has been done, but I recognize that there are structural failures that make it difficult to calculate the government's efficiency in fighting this scourge by simply looking at the number of people in prison. Government institutions were created for the new system but born into the old; they still don't have all the necessary laws to make their work possible under the new constitution.

I will give you an example. Right after the government got started, I remember I ordered the investigation of a general who had been the army chief of staff. The crimes he had committed were so blatant that they were able to send him to prison while he was still on active duty. Then I remember the opposition-controlled media began their attack on us, saying it was a political trial because that general is former president Caldera's son-in-law. That man spent about two months in prison and then a judge exonerated him entirely, claiming there was insufficient proof of his guilt.

Another example from the beginning of my government is when I told the Political Police to look into various cases of suspected corruption and we began to move forward with the investigations. One night the head of the DISIP calls me and says, "We caught a group of people our government appointed to the Hippodrome red-handed, blackmailing, trying to buy someone off with a lot of cash, and we have pictures to prove it." But what happened? The celebration ended quickly. A few days into the trial, the judge let them go. The photos were insufficient proof because the defendants argued that the police planted the money to implicate them, and there was no way to prove that they had brought the money to the table.

As the executive branch, we have initiated hundreds of investigations, which we have sent to the corresponding police units. I have personally asked government functionaries, some who were close to me, to step down because of accusations and some evidence of corruption. These cases are then investigated either by a commission of the National Assembly, the judicial branch, or the comptroller, and it is at that level that things get held up.

On the other hand, the fight against corruption is not just about prosecution but also about prevention; it is a pedagogical, educational task. My government has taken action that clearly demonstrates our commitment to fighting against the scourge of corruption. I don't know if you are aware, but in Venezuela all the intelligence agencies—the DISIP, the DIM, the PTJ, and some ministries—maintained secret expense accounts.

There was an old rule that allowed for expenses like feeding the troops, buying uniforms, shoes, combat boots, hats, for example, to be funded from secret accounts, so that these expenses—millions of dollars—could be maintained at the discretion of a few officers, with little or no oversight. These secret expenses were one of the largest sources of corruption in the country, not only for the military but also for civilians. What did we do about all this? We reformed the procedures and reduced the money going into secret accounts by almost 80 percent and along with it the corruption those accounts engendered.

That is one of the most effective policies we have implemented. We reduced those expenses so much that we actually created new problems. For example, intelligence agencies often don't have the resources to purchase their equipment: mini-microphones, telescopes, etc. Previously they didn't require permission from anybody to make those purchases; the money was there and you spent it however you liked. And that is precisely how, over time, the people in charge of secret accounts amassed fortunes of millions and millions of dollars of embezzled state money. All the big arms contracts—tanks, planes, missiles, bombs, all that was out of secret accounts…. Can you imagine?

But that major step in fighting corruption went practically unnoticed, and we failed to publicize it.

The attorney general and the comptroller's offices are the central government bodies in the fight against corruption, but they both have serious limitations. In both of these bodies, there are groups of functionaries who have worked there for ages and who bring with them the bad habits of the Fourth Republic. Many of them even sabotage investigations, give the investigators false leads, are in cahoots with the people being investigated, and so forth. There are thousands of forms of corruption and as many ways to interfere with investigations into corruption.

In the attorney general's office, for example, there are still prosecutors whose contracts protect them, who have worked there for many years, and who, if you do not have extremely solid proof, you cannot remove from office. Some who have been removed have appealed to the courts, which are also weakened by holdovers from the previous regime. Some four hundred people have been fired, but there are thousands of cases.

Now that we are on the topic of institutional barriers, I am sure you know that Lenin died worried that he had been unable to change the Czarist state apparatus even after six years of revolution. Did you ever imagine that it would be so difficult to change the state apparatus that you inherited? In my studies of local governments, people who take public office learn that it is much harder to govern than they had expected. And for this reason militants who stay out of the government often distance themselves from those within the government.

Certainly controlling a state with the level of complexity, clientalism, and inadequacies that we have had and continue to have is extremely complicated. Much more so than I had imagined it would be. There are tons of organizations, or state bodies, that we were not familiar with. Remember that we created a map of the state to note the different institutions and the people who controlled them, but institutions keep appearing. And if you add the habits and the vices of their particular public functionaries.... Can you believe that they still haven't changed an old law that protects the client bureaucrats that the AD and COPEI parties incorporated into the government? The law prevents a minister, or any high functionary, from removing these holdovers. There have been cases where some ministers have removed people in their ministry and then been forced to rehire them.

The first days in office I found situations that were unimaginable. The first problem we faced was that there was no money even to pay salaries. Oil was at around seven dollars per barrel and the budget that they left us with—further weakened by inflation—had been written based on a $14 per barrel base. Because of the "Chávez threat," the country's "risk" went through the roof. No one wanted to lend us a penny. In the middle of the constitutional assembly I had to travel the world looking for international support. I went to China, to Saudi Arabia, to several Latin American countries. I got close to Fernando Henrique Cardoso and with Brazil as a whole. There were so many bureaucratic obstacles to making even the smallest changes. Why? Because we found ourselves with a series of laws, codes, and rules that made the necessary steps more difficult. To transfer resources to a particular ministry, for example, they had to come with I don't know how many folders for me to sign. To authorize retirements, functionaries had to go through an entire bureaucratic process. We have also had to go up against the traditional culture, resistance to change.

What happens a lot of times is you assign a public servant with good skills to go to a particular institution and transform it, but the institution ends up sucking him in, swallowing him. Take the massive PDVSA company, for example. We have yet to achieve significant changes there.

We have achieved significant change at the macro-structural level with the new constitution. In the executive branch, for example, we made several changes at the highest levels: we reduced the ministries, merged a few. We also made mistakes in that area, for example, when we merged the ministry of agriculture with the ministry of production, commerce, and tourism into one super ministry. Now, three years later, we have had to separate agriculture and land. We eliminated I don't know how many foundations. There were an infinite number of funds, even a fund to study the green grub on corn in the state of Portuguesa, things like that....

Now, in terms of transforming the ministries from within, we have not made enough progress. Those inflexible, difficult, complicated structures have held us back. But I think we are on the right path. It does require a healthy dose of good will and the capacity to transform these structures and create an appropriate legal infrastructure. We will not be able to accomplish much until they change the "Law of the Civil Servant", that old law which I have been telling you about, which protects bureaucrats who are no longer necessary.

What lessons have you learned from this process of institutional struggle that might be useful for the Left, for progressives? If you could do it all over again, what would you change and what would you do the same?

I think that a movement like ours should have selected and prepared a large number of the new state employees in anticipation of our victory in the 1998 elections, and we did not do that. As a result, there was a lot of improvisation, which led to errors including appointing suboptimal people to government positions. I think that a party like ours, that has a real chance of rising to power, should look for resources for the future government, and begin preparing the members who will take office to work efficiently in their new posts, even while in the midst of the electoral campaign. This process must be meticulous, and carefully planned to include training courses and so on. One would have to do what armies do when they train their cadres, giving them physical discipline, battle orientation, and strategy. We did not do that and it was a grave mistake, especially since the people handing over the government operations were not from our party.

And even more so when they are inclined to sabotage the new government...

They lost files, burned things. Hardly any of the primary state employees wanted to accept the transition of government or give access to the necessary information to the people who were assigned to take up their position. In that area, we lacked foresight and planning, and we still have grave deficiencies in terms of our training of public employees. We need a good school to train public officials.

Marta, I believe that one must distinguish between the constitution and state institutions. I think that the situation that is arising may force us strategically to revise the operations of the government's branches.

We have, for example, the case of the electoral branch. Today, that branch is practically incapacitated. In over six months it has been unable to produce a final verdict with regard to CTV elections and there is evidence of electoral fraud on the part of Aristóbulo Istúriz— who was candidate for the presidency of CTV—and María Cristina Iglesias, who was his campaign chief. There have been similar accusations against other groups, but this body of five people has not been able to come to an agreement or make a decision. This is evidence that an apparatus of the state as important as the electoral branch has totally stagnated.

In addition to the weaknesses in the National Assembly—as I was saying earlier—caused by our failure to maintain a strategic alliance with parties like the PPT, several legislators who were elected with the MVR have turned and are now against the government. One has to realize that in a process of profound change, people also change: the process is radicalized and you realize that there are legislators who have stayed behind and who no longer represent the political positions of the people who elected them. I should have been much more demanding than I was during the campaign in terms of my opinion on legislative candidates. Today, some of the people who were elected to the National Assembly with our support are enemies of the people, and are involved in corruption. The same thing is true with governors and mayors. Look at what has happened with the mayor of the greater metropolitan area of Caracas, Alfredo Peña, for example. He was elected with my support and is now one of my main opponents; the people of Caracas feel betrayed. And the same thing has happened in other parts of the country. The people voted for some politicians who went on the campaign trail in the name of Bolívar and under the flag of the MVR and a few months later these same people changed their positions.

Then add to that the fact that once the opposition failed in their violent attempt to get me out of office, they took the initiative via the institutional route. They are using a diverse array of methods to try to tip the balance of power in the National Assembly. With a majority they might be able to remove the attorney general, a key player in their strategy of an institutional coup because the attorney general is the only one who can authorize legal action against the president. But the attorney general has stood firm in spite of all they have done to denigrate his name, intimidate him, and threaten his family.

How do you resolve this issue of the representatives who have abandoned their electorate, the people who have been elected by a particular popular mandate and have ended up betraying that mandate, changing their colors?

There is the constitutional recourse known as the recall referendum. Some people have been talking about using that recourse to get me out of office. This is laid out in the constitution, but before me will come many others. My recall will have to be the last one because it will be after August 19, 2003,[9] but they could begin on February 14, 2003, with the legislators. We will see what happens with those representatives who made it into the assembly locked arm in arm with me and are now out there talking about how I should leave the government. They promised loyalty until death and at the first opportunity betrayed us all.

We realize that the referendum process could force a few of our mayors and governors out of office. It is a risk. It forces the governors to assume their responsibilities because halfway through their term, the same people who elected them can fire them.

And what will happen with the cases against the people who participated in the military coup?

As I was explaining, the new constitution has certain clauses that provide for a general, or an admiral—without exception—to be tried, but first the case has to be shown to have merit—prima facie grounds to move forward. The attorney general of the Republic already prepared the initial case against the members of the military who participated in the coup and handed over a massive file to the

Supreme Court, which will decide whether there is enough evidence to merit bringing those men to trial. If we did not go through that process, then we would be violating the constitution. There is sufficient evidence against a group of generals and admirals in terms of their role in the attempted coup but the opposition's extensive resources and support network for the accused has delayed the verdict of the Supreme Court. I am confident that justice will be served, and not only amongst the military participants, but also the civilians. This is what most Venezuelans are hoping for. This is a trial by fire for all those structurally flawed institutions.

But, let's assume for a minute that a minority who uses pressure to obtain a majority takes the Supreme Court hostage, or that it is controlled from outside the court itself, so that instead of administering justice it misadministers it, instead of bringing the people who participated in the coup to trial, it brings the president of the Republic, as some have suggested and begun working toward. In that case, the country, not only the constitution, but the whole country, the huge percentage of Venezuelans that continue to support me, the revolutionary project, would have to help find a solution that we hope would be peaceful, democratic, in line with the constitution. It could be a referendum because the constitution allows for amendments by referendum.[10] And we have already begun to consider this as a way to get around the current situation—to reform a few articles in the constitution, using the majority we have in the National Assembly and that we are trying to strengthen. And a form of recourse of last resort is to convene another constitutional assembly, but we did that just three years ago and so we would have to try the amendment, reform route first.

The constitution might have a lot of weaknesses and holes, but one of its amazing qualities, and there are many, is that it stabilizes the structures that prevent the constituents' power from being expropriated from the people. In the case of an institutional political crisis with no apparent solution, there is always one last resort: that the people, collecting enough signatures, or the National Assembly, or the president of the Republic can call for a referendum to reform, amend, restructure, or even reframe the constitution. Obviously, to rewrite the constitution entirely the other measures would have had to have been exhausted.

At the end of the day, what do you make of this process?

In spite of all of the difficulties we are experiencing, I am pleased. And I believe that the right-wing reaction against us reveals that they feel that the process, albeit limited, is truly striking at the heart of the long-standing status quo. If they did not feel truly threatened, they would not have resorted to these kinds of tactics. This means that more important than how many obstacles, how many micro or medium structures stay intact or barely afloat, is the fact that our project is strategically oriented and on the right track. I believe that we have the strength to continue advancing, to continue deconstructing with the one hand and constructing with the other. We leaders must be able to recognize that strength and not think we are weak or that we have to begin to retreat, to throw in the towel. The strength is there; this was made clear on April 11, 2002, and we can build it up further both in terms of quantity and in terms of quality. There is a whole world out there to improve, to organize; we must increase the level of consciousness, of organization, so that we do not waste our strength and instead build the capacity to transform.

Simón Rodríguez said in one of his writings, "Material force is in the masses; moral force is in the movement." And I dare to add: "The transformative power of the masses is in an accelerated and highly conscious political movement."

CHAPTER THREE

The Military in the Revolution and the Counterrevolution

Many times I have had to defend you against those who criticize you for surrounding yourself with the military. I understand the anguish of the leader of a government who must quickly resolve fundamental problems but cannot count on a state apparatus to rise to the occasion or on party members to be sufficiently prepared. I think this is what has driven you to look for support from the military. But then it seems that there is a contradiction between the fact that the main executors of the most important tasks of the revolutionary process are the military and that this process is conceived as one in which the sovereign people exercise power through participation at every level. I understand that the military is often efficient and disciplined, but it's not accustomed to giving up power; it's not prepared to encourage people to participate.

I have heard that, in this sense, Plan Bolívar 2000 has meant many good things for people—roads, schools, houses—concrete solutions, but they are solutions that come from above without people's participation. On the other hand, I'm convinced that participation cannot be decreed; people need to learn how to participate. It's a slow cultural transformation process. What can you say about this?

Let's suppose that this criticism—which I have heard before even in party meetings—is completely true, in the sense that the military only knows how to give and execute orders, that they are executives who are not inclined to allow participation. This is not really true. Take me for example. Ever since I was young, my focus was on participation and I had wonderful experiences when I was the commander of units with remote postings, especially in small towns where we launched participatory actions that were very good lessons and that conflicted with the local political power. "Why is this soldier sticking his nose where it doesn't belong, fixing roads and playing baseball with the people?" And I am not the only one who favors participation. If that were the case, I would have clashed with a closed, authoritarian and nonparticipatory military structure; I would not have lasted in the army.

Now, you are right when you say that there is a strong military presence in my government. Imagine February 2, 1999, with almost all the state and municipal governments opposing us; the Congress against us; the Supreme Court against us; a budget written by the previous regime; a government almost without resources to pay salaries; the price of oil down to seven dollars per barrel; on top of this, pressure from the high expectations our electoral triumph had generated: around the palace there were lines of thousands of people asking for jobs, with their sick kids, sleeping there, on the ground, not letting my car pass. "We are not leaving until Chávez sees us." Now add a party structure engaged in the political struggle; the constitutional assembly was coming, all of that was coming. So I decided to turn to the Armed Force. Without the participation of the military in the social arena through Plan Bolívar 2000 [initiated in 1999 and continuing through 2000], the process would not have advanced in its political arena as quickly as it did.

This is how Plan Bolívar 2000, a civilian-military plan, was born. My order to my men was: "Go house to house combing the land. Hunger is the enemy." And we started on February 27, 1999, ten years after the *Caracazo*, as a way of redeeming the military. I even made the connection when I said, "Ten years ago we came out to massacre the people, now we are going to fill them with love. Go and comb the land, search out and destroy poverty and death. We are going to fill them with life instead of lead." And the response was really beautiful.

While we, the politicians, were engaged in the political struggle, 40,000 soldiers were on a campaign to attend to the health of the people—opening roads with military engineering equipment, flying passengers in military planes to the poorest areas, charging them just at cost.

I told each of the military leaders: "Show me your plan based on your resources and capacity." And each unit of the Armed Force started outlining its plan. The air force and its plan of social routes: helicopters and military planes flying where no roads existed with passengers who carried their chickens and little boxes. The navy and Plan Pescar 2000: they have been involved with the fishermen, organizing cooperatives, repairing iceboxes and refrigerators, giving fishermen courses, etc. We gave the national guard mainly the task of protecting the citizens and controlling petty crime, but also [to implement] programs all over the country, even in indigenous areas that had previously never been served. I hope you can go there to see for yourself. There are things that seem like miracles. That is not to deny mistakes and even corruption in some of the military, especially in the higher ranks, and the sabotage of the opposition. But the guys have developed an impressive social conscience.

The guard came up with Plan Casiquiare 2000. Casiquiare is a river in the jungle, which has thousands of indigenous people inhabiting its shores. They even built a boat to go from village to village, bringing medicines and doctors to examine children and administer vaccinations, building houses with the indigenous people under the direction of the people themselves, not a top-down process.

Then, projects like Barranco Yopal and Caravali started to arise with the Cuiva and Yaruro peoples. Many years ago I used to go to Barranco Yopal, taking sheet metal and poles to the natives, because with those materials they built winter huts, which they left during the summer. They were nomads: hunters and gatherers, as they have been for five hundred years. I saw native women give birth there, squatting on a hill, throwing away the placenta and cleaning the baby, and then keep walking. Many of those children died of malaria, tuberculosis, or other diseases. They were troubled, drunk most of the time in the village. The native women prostituted themselves, and many were raped. They were ghosts, most of the population scorned them. They sometimes had to steal in order to eat. They did not have the same concept of private property; for them, to steal a pig for food because they were hungry was not considered robbery. But what do I see there now? The military with an agricultural technician and their skill at mobilizing vehicles, equipment, organization, speed; but with the native capitanes [indigenous leader] leading, wearing hats reading "Plan Bolívar." The soldiers carried the materials, helped them with some engineering personnel and manpower more than anything, while the natives outlined the houses and worked building their schools and houses. Whose idea was it that the people should participate and not just receive...?

The military came up with the idea, along with agricultural technicians and engineers. Plan Bolívar has not only been military—each garrison has contracted civilian technicians who specialize in that particular kind of work.

Well, then, those natives were happy, it showed in their faces. They took me to see their crops. On only four hectares they were producing sugarcane, watermelons, bananas, corn, papayas. They were eating well and now they were asking for a truck to take their produce to the village to sell it. They had already received small boats with motors and training in their use—before they used to fish with harpoons, with spears from the shores of small rivers. I went fishing with them a couple of times. They used to fish with their bare hands or with big stones. That community was resuscitated.

Once I gave a speech in that region. I used a saying from *Zarathustra*. I said, "Fifteen years ago I came here and I saw you with your ashes. Now I am back and I see you with your fire."

We also have Plan Wasp, which is really encouraging participation. General García Carneiro invented the plan. One day he came to me with his plan. "What is this?" I said. "Are you going to vaccinate people?" "No, my friend," he replied. "It is about people building their own houses on their own isolated plots of land." "Alright, let's hear it." And they showed me some illustrations. "Look how they used to live," he said, and showed me a photograph of a family standing in front of a hut made out of wooden poles and sheet metal. "And look two months later. The same family, now better off, with a house." Who built that house? The community built it. While a private company builds one of those houses for ten million *bolívares*, Plan Wasp does it for three million [approximately US$5,000 and $1,500, respectively]. Why? Because it is the community that builds the houses. And that, at the same time, allows us to create employment. The soldiers obtained machines to make cinder blocks and they give courses with civilian technicians and masons. They also make wooden doors. With INCE (National Institute of Educational Cooperation)—to which I appointed a retired general who is a very demanding and extremely efficient man; I know him well because he was my teacher—they were able to build forty mobile classrooms for technical education. If the trailers did not have tires, or if they were broken down, we gave them money to repair them. We got a loan from Spain for new equipment and other supplies. Now we have all those portable classrooms rolling across the country. They arrive in a town; they give their courses and teach people how to make doors. Then, together they make the doors, the building blocks, the roof tiles, and build the houses. Corruption is minimal. We can't say zero, but it is decreasing significantly.

Where did this come from? From the heart of Plan Bolívar and certainly not only from the military, but from those members of the military who are in touch with reality, from the soldier who understands that resources alone are not enough to build houses. People begin to talk, to calculate, and from that dialogue Plan Wasp is born.

In one town, a group from the army finished building a highway that had been under construction for more than twenty years. The budget to finish it with asphalt and everything else that was needed was around five billion bolívares. With the military machinery and the military engineers, they were able to complete the job with only 1.5 billion. That means the cost of many of the public works—housing, highways, bridges, roads—went down. We completed a gigantic national operation.

And regarding health care, don't get me started. We organized a formidable voluntary medical network and began using military hospitals to provide operations; it was a social war on disease. There were lines of people. Once, in a town named Zaraza, military and civilian personnel from Plan Bolívar operated on more people—eye operations, leg operations—than the hospital of that town had performed in the previous ten years. A very impressive performance! I remember that once one of those guys said, "You have to see how beautiful it is to give eyesight back to an old man, see him crying out of happiness, and hear him saying, 'To think that I believed that I was going to die without seeing the blue sky again.' That is what makes us happy, feel useful." This contact with the people unleashed a flood of feelings and desire to participate.

The governor of the state of Cojedes—a large prairie state south of Caracas, almost at the center of the country—is a lieutenant-colonel in the national guard who did not participate in any of the uprisings. He was the military chief of Plan Bolívar in that state right in the midst of the constitutional process. When the election process for governor started, he came to me one day and said, "Look, Mr. President, I want to submit my resignation." "Why, *muchacho*, you are only a lieutenant-colonel?" "Well, the parties of the revolution here are asking me to be gubernatorial candidate in order to defeat the *adecos*."[1] "Are you sure about that?" After a few days I received a letter signed by the MVR and other leaders of the leftist parties from that state. With his candidacy we even solved a problem that had seemed insoluble: internal divisions. This guy was able to bring them all together, we won the elections, and now he is governor. He revealed himself as a leader. Of course, he and his guards spent a lot of time in the villages, in the countryside, serving the people and that's how they started to view him as a leader. There are many cases like this one. I have mentioned only a few.

And look, many political leaders have come up short when compared with the military personnel. Some of them get jealous, because when it comes time to step up and play a leadership role, a lot of the politicians find themselves surpassed by a guy who learned leadership skills as I described earlier, in the military.

There are many good examples, and of course we also have a few bad ones. But the accumulation of the good ones is marvelous and exceeds the errors and defects of the few bad apples. Suspicious behavior is sent to the comptroller's office for investigation. The comptroller told me a few days ago that he has found that Plan Bolívar—which started with problems—is one of the plans that has improved the most.

What errors are you referring to?

For example, the money planned to solve one problem was used to solve another. These budgets are strictly controlled: if twenty million *bolívares* are allocated to repair housing, it cannot be diverted for other expenses.

I remember once, in the midst of a gathering crowd, a crying woman emerged carrying a child with a dislocated leg. He looked like a rag doll. A big kid, seven or eight years old, who couldn't walk. I saw her and was deeply moved. I stopped and stepped out of the car with the general chief of the garrison who also served as the head of Plan Bolívar. The woman told me that the child was born like that and that she had never had the money for surgery. "Come here, general, write down the address. Arrange for him to have an operation." Then, someone had to pay for the surgery. Another time someone needed a prosthetic limb, and so on. Someone had to pay and so they took the money from whichever account without keeping good records. Some did it out of inexperience, while others were taking advantage of the system.

Then, because at the beginning the comptroller's office was in the hands of the opposition, they started using these situations to campaign against me. When the news broke—"Corruption in Plan Bolí-

–I thought that they destroyed the plan. Imagine! The press, try-
destroy all our projects, came out with a list that included the
names of all the supposedly corrupt members of the military. I called
some of them and told them that they had to justify the expenses to
the last bolívar. Then we opened an investigation: they had to find the
guy with the leg, where had they paid for his prosthesis. Invoice after
invoice was scrutinized. That way, almost everything was justified.
Some cases are pending; others have been closed.

*Obviously, a lot of people ended up with the initial information from
the press and never knew the results of the investigations. It's terrible
how baseless campaigns are launched and then, when the data gathered demonstrate the falsehood of the accusations, the media doesn't
publish corrections and if they do, they bury them in the back of the
paper so that nobody notices.*

That's how it goes. But, back to the plan. The comptroller determined that in 1999 and 2000 Plan Bolívar accomplished 280 percent of its target goals.

This year, for instance, we haven't been able to allocate resources
for Plan Bolívar. So they are finishing projects left pending from last
year, like the project that we witnessed today.[2] Now the plan is in
another stage, the one we call "entering the structure." There are no
longer hundreds of soldiers in the streets. I already have governors,
mayors, plans in action, government structure. It's no longer the
government of three years ago; therefore the military is limited to
coordinating special projects with local and regional governments.
They are no longer leading these projects by themselves.

There are units that have returned to the garrison to dedicate
themselves full time to their routine training activities—we had
even gotten to the point of putting combat units to work on the
plan—because we need combat units to train for combat: infantry
battalions, submariners, paratroopers, etc. So, a lot of these units
have returned to their routine training functions.

We're also organizing reserve units. What does that consist of?
We bring together guys who had already been in the Armed Force,

most of them unemployed youth without specialized education, without professional skills, to form cooperatives. In 2001 we organized eight thousand of those guys and they started to form cooperatives. The same idea: cooperatives, micro credits, donations of land; we have even transferred state assets that were idle in the hands of FOGADE (Bank Deposits Guarantee Fund). When we had a serious banking crisis, many bankers fled the country, but they left a lot of assets behind. The state appropriated the assets because they were deposit guarantees. Many have been sold to recover capital, but there was still land and abandoned factories. We have been transferring these remaining assets to some groups of reservists to enable them to form cooperatives. They receive agriculture courses and start working.

This is part of Plan Bolívar: to organize the reserves—the people—and give them some necessary tools. Plan Pescar [Fishing] 2000 is also making progress. It has already accumulated capital and established fishing cooperatives in collaboration with the navy. The navy supports them, arrives at their wharves, and helps them repair engines. The national guard is working together with indigenous people on the frontiers.

Marta, what happened on April 12 and 13 is directly related to the civilian-military process we have been talking about. In spite of its failures and above and beyond the social attention and participation that was at stake in Plan Bolívar, the primary goal has been accomplished: a civilian-military alliance. What happened on April 12 had never happened before in this country: hundreds of thousands of unarmed Venezuelans, many of them without political organization or party affiliations, without a preconceived plan, headed through the streets to the barracks and surrounded them en masse. They sang the national anthem. They spoke to the soldiers and yelled to them: *"¡Soldado, consciente, busca a tu presidente!"* [Soldier, with conscience, go find your president!] and *"¡Soldado, amigo, el pueblo está contigo!"* [Soldier, friend, with the people to the end!] Not only did they go to Fort Tiuna, but they also went to barracks all over the country. Nothing like that had ever happened before in Venezuela, and it wasn't because I was in those barracks. In fact, the masses that surrounded Fort Tiuna on the third day, when it was already publicly known that I wasn't there, were impressive: 300,000 people or more.

This also happened in places like Maracay, where soldiers from the paratroopers brigade saw people outside the barracks. They said, "More people are needed, we need more people to join us," and they went to the neighborhoods to recruit more civilian support. Of course, they know the community leaders and those leaders know them, because each military unit had been assigned a particular area. Such-and-such battalion corresponded to such-and-such neighborhood. They have been doing that for three years—the military goes to the neighborhoods, does patrols, builds a school, or fixes a medical clinic. These units already had established good reputations with their respective communities. This represented quite a change, because after the February 27 massacre, for instance, to go to a poor neighborhood a soldier had to dress as a civilian. He was taking a risk, because the army had massacred the people. Today, when a soldier shows up, people greet him with enthusiasm and happiness.

This popular uprising would not have happened without the profound contact and cooperation between the army and the people. That is Mao's theory. The water and the fish. The people are to the army what the water is to the fish. In Venezuela today we have fish in the water and that is why the opposition is campaigning against Plan Bolívar, to try to break, fracture that unity. A good part of the military is with the people. Of course, there are sectors of the military that are opposed; they echo the hollow rhetoric of the opposition. What is this rhetoric? That I am going to destroy the Armed Force, that the plan negatively affects the operative capacity of the Armed Force because now the military is cleaning the sewers. The opposition and the few military leaders that are with them go on the radio, in the newspapers, at home and abroad and spew this hollow rhetoric. However, on the ground, the response to the plan is clearly positive. Today, I saw soldiers working for Plan Bolívar in Puerto Cruz, with Bercerra, a navy captain, and they were happy to see the school they had been working on with locals finished.

Regarding the peaceful aspect of the revolution, when you'v[
asked if you fear that a new Chile might happen in your co[
you've answered that there are significant differences between tnc
Chilean process and this process. Before I develop that further, I want-
ed to point out that in 1973, when the coup in Chile happened, you
were in the Venezuelan mountains training young military cadets.
While there, you heard the words of Fidel Castro who denounced the
coup and [mourned]Allende's death. He said something else that was
permanently engraved in your mind: "If every worker, if every laborer
had had a rifle in their hands, the fascist coup in Chile would not have
happened." This prescient reflection allows us to better understand the
differences between the Chilean revolution and the process here in
Venezuela. You have said that the Chilean revolution was unarmed
while the Bolivarian Revolution has arms and people ready to use
them if necessary to defend Venezuela's sovereignty. On the other hand,
before the coup in April 2002, you said that any coup attempt could
radicalize the revolution, therefore the oligarchy had better think seri-
ously about taking that step. You've also affirmed that having a mili-
tary force doesn't necessarily mean "using the arms" but rather count-
ing on them as "a supporting and dissuading force."[3] *In fact, accord-*
ing to your account, the Armed Force blocked an attempted military
coup during the 1998 elections and also detected and prevented elec-
toral fraud during the same elections. One cannot deny that they've
played an important role during the current process: first, as guaran-
tors of six elections/referendums in less than two years, detecting fraud
and military coups; second, as the main executors of Plan Bolívar
2000 and of the emergency relief efforts in the wake of the natural
disasters that recently hit many parts of Venezuela.

I understand that before the April 11, 2002, coup, you counted
on the support of the majority of those in high command, despite the
fact that in the previous few months some high-ranking officials
publicly asked you to resign as president of the Republic, and Gen-
eral Guaicaipuro Lameda had recently resigned as president of
the state-owned Petróleos de Venezuela (PDVSA). He reportedly
disagreed with government policy.

Nonetheless, the coup on April 11 was only possible because an important sector of the high-ranking officers supported the opposition, although it's also true that the majority of the officers continue to support you and that their support made possible your return to power.

How do you explain your misreading of your level of support within the Armed Force? And this gets at the heart of a larger topic: how does a national leader obtain objective information on what is going on in his country? The people around him, in order to please him, to save him worries or because of opportunism, often avoid informing him of the real problems by giving him an optimistic analysis. Some leaders simply fail to pay attention to critical information. Is there any mechanism to avoid what Eduardo Galeano has called the "echo problem"?

Or as Matus says: "The leader and his bell jar."

In regard to the first question, without any doubt I overestimated the strength of a group of people whom I believed I knew well enough. When feelings play an important role it is sometimes fatal, tragic. Since 1999, I continued respecting the military hierarchy with minor variations. There was no major shakeup of the military leadership. And I was clearly wrong with regard to their respect for the constitution, the government, the commander-in-chief. In reality, I wasn't totally mistaken; if I had been, you and I wouldn't be sitting here. In reality the response on the Saturday following the coup that allowed the government to return to power shows in a very objective manner that the great majority of the generals were not involved. A minority was able to mislead the rest. I was suspicious of some of them. There was no surprise regarding those who engineered the coup. We had some information about, for instance, the military attaché in Washington and some intelligence on other generals. But I admit that I was wrong regarding some persons in key positions, like the commander-in-chief of the army, General Vázquez Velasco, and that I never even thought that a group of officers was able to reach such extremes as to get involved with the coup. Here, I am self-critical and I have learned to be much more cautious.

General Guaicaipuro Lameda's resignation had a really negative effect on the situation. Many members of the military were surprised by the way the situation was managed, but did not show it until later.

In any case, it's been a learning experience. From now on we're going to pay much more attention to certain signals, we're going to try to be more precise in our evaluations of every single human being—their interests, the internal conflicts of the particular institution, often in the context of outside agitation.

Now, with regard to the second question on how a leader can obtain accurate information about what is going on in the country, I don't doubt that a leader needs a team that constantly follows current events and informs him without manipulating the reality, without covering up information. Now, it's true what you said, that for different reasons the information given to the head of state is often not sufficiently clear, and I think this is unavoidable. What do I do in order to correct that situation? I read the papers, which is one way of staying informed. I particularly like to rummage through the inside pages where denunciations, letters from the public, and the readers' page are printed. I read up and then I start calling my people. "Look, what happened with this?" "What kind of problem is that?"

On the other hand, I have a group of people, some are military, others civilian, which I call the *Inspectoría*. I send them to do unannounced inspections on some particular sites; I ask them to bring me information about what they find along with photographs and reports. In this way I collect valuable information on how well various projects and agencies are working. I insist that they tell me the truth. I insist that the chief of intelligence tell me the facts, the details, the moment he gets his information. Obviously, my informants have to use their judgment because the president doesn't need to be overwhelmed by rumors, by information circulating on the streets, but he needs to be informed of those facts that may impact his decision making. It's a constant predicament of mine. And I think we are improving in this area.

And, Marta, I tend to run away from the confinement of the bell jar that Matus refers to in order to have direct contact with the people. I receive a huge amount of papers and letters. Naturally, I don't have time to read them all, but I do read a fair amount of them, and the guys who work with me read, process, and give me abstracts. That way many complaints from different areas—social, economic, and popular—reach me. I have contact with small groups such as the one in Las Malvinas, with sixty leaders from the neighborhood who inform, criticize, make suggestions, present preliminary projects and ideas. Other times, walking on the streets, I ask random people questions. All these are mechanisms, some institutional, others personal, for obtaining an objective picture of the political and structural situation.

I'm aware that this cannot be limited to personal, spasmodic actions. It must be a continuing process with a methodology that allows us to diagnose, evaluate, and inspect. We need to organize an office capable of detecting problems and following instructions. This is the best way of staying informed at the highest level possible—it would be terrible to be deceived, to end up blind to the world, thinking that everything is fine while the country is going up in smoke.

And in relation to your consulting team, do you aim to surround yourself with people who are critical? Do you readily accept criticism?

Yes, of course, and I actually ask for it. I don't like complacent people. If there are decisions being made that a minister or official does not agree with, it seems to me absolutely crucial that the issue be discussed, deliberated on, so that we reach the best policy.

Do you believe that the military is not one homogenous group? I believe that the April 11 coup reveals that you can count on the support of the majority of the troops, the noncommissioned officers and the young officers. Those who betrayed you were essentially members of the higher ranks, the sector most susceptible to the influence of the dominant class. Is that right?

Yes, but it's also not all the generals....

How many generals took part in the coup?

Those who really participated in the coup, those who had been planning it for quite some time, and those who subscribed to the operation or manipulation and support of the coup constitute no more than 20 percent of the military, and perhaps even less. And if you analyze almost all the officers, one by one, you may understand their motivations—some political, some economic. Some, because they don't quite understand the political process, others because they're influenced by that persistent campaign that raises fears about communism, the Colombian guerilla, Bolívarian popular militias, the plan to weaken the Armed Force, et cetera. Some were confused; others were consciously engaged in the coup.

Of almost one hundred generals, that little group is no bigger than twenty, despite the fact that many of them were in the video.[4] The one who read the communiqué was among the conspirators but the majority of them were there because they had been ordered to be; they were manipulated. They were told, "The president ordered us to kill civilians and now he wants us to go to the street to continue the killings. He himself has said that the soldier who directs arms against his own people be damned (a quote from Bolívar). Therefore we're not going to obey his orders; we're going to declare ourselves institutionally." And many of them fell into that game, that trap, that manipulation.

How would you characterize the group involved with the coup?

Almost all the conspirators are men of privilege, with political contacts with the previous government, with AD and COPEI, or officers who had become wealthy, sometimes through shady business deals in association with "dogs of war." There were "dogs of war" involved in the coup: Mr. Pérez Recao, weapons and military equipment dealer.

I continue thinking, despite what happened, that the majority, even among the generals—people of my generation—did not participate in the coup.

*What is your analysis of what happened within the Armed Force?
How was it possible that the military you trusted were won over for
the coup attempt?*

Venezuela is living a historical conflict—that's how we categorize it—
it's a break from the past. One cannot ignore a sector with historical,
social, economic, psychological ties to society as a whole. So the
Armed Force has been feeling the impact of the national shakeup for
quite some time already. It's not a sector isolated from national events.

And within this context a group of military officers, obviously
shaped by a certain understanding of democracy, were co-opted,
convinced by groups of civilians, politicians, and businessmen to
support the coup. They are people who spent one, two, or more
decades immersed in a process with external influences that generated individual or group interests very similar to the interests of the
civilian, political, and business sectors. Some of those officers were
engaged; they were the promoters of the coup and for many years
they belonged to groups that took shape and [gained] shelter within the established power structure. They accumulated privileges or
took over privileged positions. When our revolution arrived and
our government took power, they started to lose their privileges,
such as the control of the armed institutions and contracts for military purchasing. Therefore, it's not surprising that Isaac Pérez
Recao, one of those involved in the coup who is now in the United
States, is a man who for many years did business selling weapons:
rifles, grenades, and armored vehicles to the Armed Force. This
man befriended, for instance, one of our generals in Washington.
The day of the coup, that general [Enrique Medina Gómez] came
back from Washington on Pérez Recao's plane and joined the conspirators. He even smuggled weapons—but not weapons that
belonged to the Venezuelan Armed Force—into Fort Tiuna.

Others had aspirations of becoming military chiefs, because
they were associated with the parties that governed the country for
a long time. They aspired to climb the ranks and, well, their plans
did not work out. And it was then that their resentment started:

"Chávez promoted another one, but not me." "Chávez is giving positions to his friends, but not to us who have the potential." All the usual stuff. They were basically—with some exceptions—the officers who became the engines of the conspiracy and who manipulated a group of lower officers.

Last night [June 12, 2002] I spoke to four air force generals who we decided not to bring to court—I've been speaking to many generals one by one; almost every week I speak to a group—and one of them explained to me that one of the generals involved in the coup told him to report to the command at the Carlota base. He followed his orders, and there he was told: "Look, do you know what's going on? Watch these images. There's a peaceful demonstration and look at the president's people, the armed Bolívarian Circles, and pay close attention, they're shooting, killing people." They showed that footage, the video that everybody saw. "The president went crazy, and now he's asking us to go out to massacre people but we're not going to do that. Do you agree?" "Well, yes, I agree. I don't want to kill people. What's going on is horrible." Moreover, he was told, "Look, the president has resigned and there is a vacuum of power. We're writing a document; we're going to declare our intentions to the country." Then a television camera captures one of the generals reading the document. He was manipulated with lies and fell into the trap. He told me: "I was stupid, but they're never going to fool me again!" And I believe him, because we have identified those who really were the instigators and we know that there's another group that was fooled, manipulated as well.

It bodes well that the following day some of them started reacting, thinking more calmly, seeing the reality and assuming appropriate positions. That was before my return. I want to clarify this to you because people might think that it was because of my return that they jumped back to my side. No, no, although some did. It was the following day that the majority reacted; they realized that I had not resigned and they took a stand in defense of democracy. Some of them did it in a more reserved manner, but in the end there were their public statements along with the people in the streets that allowed us to defeat the coup.

One of the generals involved in the coup, for instance, was the chief of Caldera's *Casa Militar* and a very good friend of Caldera's son-in-law. Another one of them is a retired general who was active when I won the elections and tried and failed to organize a coup d'état against me then. He didn't have the power to get it off the ground back in December 1998. There are a variety of reasons—some individual, others political—that brought those officers together with political parties, such as Acción Democrática and COPEI, business sectors, weapons dealers, and the corporate media. They managed to come out on top during a tumultuous moment instigated by outside agitation, and conflicts like the one affecting PDVSA. It was in the context of this that they had been preparing, for quite some time already, the events of April 11.

You say that you decided not to take them to court. What is the reason for such a benevolent attitude? You should know that there is a concern inside as well as outside Venezuela that no one is punished, that despite the fact that this is a government that has strongly opposed corruption no corrupt person has been tried in spite of the obvious evidence of corruption. The same goes for the coup d'état. I understand that some sectors of troops and noncommissioned officers who are completely engaged in the revolutionary process do not understand the government's policy in this area. Nor do they understand why you appointed General Rincón, who announced your resignation, to become minister of defense. All this gives the impression of weakness—not strength. There are those who think that the balance of forces within the Armed Force is so against you that you have no choice but to be conciliatory. How do you respond to all this?

You can interpret a situation like this one in many ways. Whether you call it weakness or strength depends on your concept of weakness and strength. After our return to power, following the coup d'état of April 11, we had many options. One was to show strength from a traditional point of view, in other words take drastic measures, like a battalion of tanks attacking, moving forward and destroying positions, flattening one wall after another, occupying space. Some people conceive of strength in that way. It's a respectable enough concept. I'm not diminishing its merit, but that doesn't mean this concept is valid for every situation. I imagine that when the Nazis were marching toward Leningrad they had this concept in mind: we're going to move forward to the heart of the enemy to blow it up. There is another concept of strength. Look at that bamboo grove. [He points to the bamboo in the garden of La Casona, the presidential residence in Caracas where this part of the interview took place.] It's an image used by the Chinese: the bamboo bends over without breaking, as opposed to other trees that seem strong but their inflexibility leads them to break. I believe I've had this concept of strength forever—the strength of flexibility, maneuvering, and intelligence, and not brute force.

Going back to what I was telling you, when I came back I had a few options. One of them was to show strength in the sense I was just talking about—if we had sent a few people to jail that would have been interpreted as strength, but we didn't do that. Some of them have left the country; others are in their homes, a few under house arrest and others without restrictions since they are under investigation.

I remember, Marta, that at the time of our uprising we were all jailed, every last one of us. We were three hundred people and there wasn't enough space for us in the jails. They had to build new prisons. The area immediately surrounding the jail where I was detained was mined because they were afraid that people would come to rescue me. We were not allowed to talk to the country for fear that we would expose the truth. In order for our wives, children, and relatives to visit us we had to write a list and send it to the Ministry of Defense so they could authorize their visit. Pablo Medina proposed that we testify before Congress and the answer was: "Certainly not! Those conspirators shouldn't be allowed to talk!" So we had to do an interview with José Vicente Rangel in Yare. The tape was smuggled out secretly but the government found out and stopped the show from going on the air. They searched my house; they even took my children's clothing and some money that belonged to my first wife. Was that a demonstration of strength? In reality, it was a demonstration of great weakness. I'm not afraid, and I couldn't care less that Carmona Estanga was in the National Assembly for, I think, fifteen or seventeen hours, being questioned, and that it was transmitted live on television and radio across the country. And that General So-and-So and Admiral So-and-So tell their version of the truth. I believe some of them ended up in a very bad position when they said, for example, "There was no coup here." People were laughing. No coup? And Carmona Estanga was saying, "There was a vacuum of power and the militaries called me and I was sworn in." Nobody, not even he himself, believes that. He made a fool of himself. People are aware of that. I believe it's been a lesson, a learning experience. Now, I don't deny that there are people, especially young and impulsive people, who may think that this is a sign of weakness and that that man shouldn't be talking, that he should be jailed in Yare, where I was detained. Perhaps you yourself share that opinion.

Now, I want to clarify something, the conspirators have not been acquitted. No, Marta, we are applying the constitution. We decided to become a political party, to get involved in elections, to win the government, to create a new constitution, to recognize five branches of government and the new constitution. As I was explaining, the new constitution has certain clauses that provide for a general, or an admiral—without exceptions—to be tried, but first the case has to be shown to have merit; there must be prima facie grounds to move forward. We decided to accept the rules of the game that we've established and that's what we're doing now.

The attorney general of the Republic already prepared the initial case against the members of the military that participated in the coup and handed over a massive file to the Supreme Court who will decide whether there is enough evidence to merit bringing those men to trial. This can't be done from one day to the next, because if one is not well prepared the case will be thrown out. One has to prepare documents, interview people. Three attorneys interviewed me for five hours; they interviewed a lot of others as well.

If we don't fulfill these steps, we would be in violation of the constitution. Of course, the comptroller's office has also taken some action. It has established some restrictions—those under investigation can't leave the country, they have to report to a probation officer, they can't make public statements, they can't participate in demonstrations.

If following the constitution is considered a sign of weakness, imagine where that would lead us! If the constitution is too permissive in some articles—and we've already detected some vulnerabilities—then it should be revised, amended if necessary. That is as valid as when one builds a house and discovers that some of its columns are weak and a decision is made to strengthen them. There are people already thinking about proposing amendments to strengthen parts of the constitution. For their part, the opposition is also demanding amendments and it's valid that they do so, that they collect signatures, in accordance with the constitutional process; after this process we have to call a referendum.

Therefore, there are different levels of responsibility for the coup. First there is a group of officers, those truly engaged in the coup d'état. They are in the pretrial phase. There's another group that we've decided not to put on trial based on a very thorough investigation, but to instead bring them to the "Council of Investigation," which is another example of the constitutional law of the Armed Force.

When you say, "We have decided," what do you mean?

I used the plural because it's not only me. I receive recommendations from the military ranks and from other sources that provide me with intelligence information. I'm in charge of gathering other information. Thus, we consolidate information in order to come closer to the truth regarding the role played by such and such soldier. This Council of Investigation is also a very serious body that can't be created from one day to the next—you can't discharge a soldier who has already reached a certain rank, and who has some rights, without clear reasons. The constitution establishes due process and the right to a defense. You have to grant him the right to defend himself; otherwise we fall into the same tendency as Carlos Andrés Pérez. He discharged a few soldiers like that, without trial or investigation. They were even taken barefoot; their weapons and everything were taken away—a humiliation. And the innocent and the guilty alike paid a price.

The men brought to the Council of Investigation are already in the final stage. About five days ago I signed a recommendation to discharge two admirals; one was the commander of the marines in Carúpano in the east and the other here in Caracas. We found that their behavior was grave but not criminal, because if the Council of Investigation determines that it was criminal, the investigation follows a longer course. The Council of Investigation is faster because it depends on the commander-in-chief. There are currently about fifteen generals and admirals from the army, the navy, the air force, and the national guard appearing before the Council of Investigation. And after that we'll decide if we should put them on trial, arrest them for a few days, admonish them verbally, or discharge them.

What I'm doing with some of them is bringing them here to talk for two or three hours and I tell them, "You made a mistake." I also tell them, "Well, look, you can keep your position, but you have to realize that you made a mistake and that if there is ever another similar situation, I hope you don't do it again." In other words, it's a moral sanction. That is within our laws and military regulations—it's what we call a "verbal admonition." I've seen a general crying here, saying, "Damn, Hugo, they fooled me, I was naïve." And I know he meant it and he told me, "Look how my children have suffered, because I was in the newspapers and my children love you very much." I've even taken on the task of publicly vindicating some of them in order to redress the moral damage done to a man with more than twenty years in the Armed Force, a man who has grandchildren, who feels like a soldier and who hurts because he was fooled when he was told that Chávez had resigned and that

Chávez killed some people. So, he said, "How could I believe that, why the hell didn't I wake up and think that this was a lie! I didn't believe my superior when he told me, but I believed the one who phoned me, and I believed the television and the whole campaign, like many others around the world."

It would be unfair if the officers who were manipulated and deceived were sent to jail. Because the only thing many of them did when they were called was to report to their commands, where they were made to stand in front of a journalist with a camera. And then one of them, the conspirator, started reading while they were standing there.

After the coup d'état we transferred some officers, in accordance with the gravity of their role in the coup. In that regard we've acted extremely carefully—we want to avoid a witch hunt within the armed forces.

One officer told me, "Look, see this photograph. We have analyzed it. The day you didn't arrive, Colonel Moreno wasn't wearing his red beret; he had a green beret. Why did he remove the red beret and put on a green beret? This may indicate that he didn't want to look like a red beret." I want to clarify that Colonel Moreno is the chief of *Casa Militar* and he was with me to the last minute of the coup d'état. I said to the officer: "Look, be careful with what you're thinking; if we're going to start doubting everybody, we're going to end up mad. That colonel risked his life that day. You're not aware of that because you were not there. Do you know why that colonel was wearing that beret? He and Colonel Morao and the soldiers under their command were all wearing green berets because, as part of the tactical plan to retake the palace, they removed their red berets since they made them easy targets. Instead, with the green berets, people who saw them didn't know which side they were on. They removed the sign that identified them as being from the Chávez regiment and the presidential guard. The guy, in good faith, doubted Colonel Moreno. But imagine that because of a misinterpreted photo, because of gossip or a comment, some officers could come under investigation for no reason.

Another one told me, "Look, Colonel So-and-So went home, nobody saw him around here the day we were planning the taking back of the palace." In fact, that colonel was in another place coordinating something else. It means that one can't let oneself be guided by impulses, by preliminary observations, and unleash—in such a complicated and sensitive environment as the Armed Force—a witch hunt.

Can you explain to me why you appointed the general who announced your resignation to the country—General Rincón— as minister of defense? Nobody can understand that. How is it possible that you can trust someone who said that you'd resigned when you had not?

There are many versions of what happened that day, but I do know the truth. Maybe I'm the only one who knows it exactly as it happened. I know what drove him to make that announcement, that he is not guilty. He is the victim of a situation in which I am also implicated, perhaps that is why I am the only one who understands his role.

Why? Did you have an ambiguous position at some point?

I wouldn't say ambiguous, but there was a moment when we in fact started to discuss the possibility of a resignation. That was when I realized that we had lost almost all our military force on hand in order to resist or move to another place. So I called José Vicente and William Lara, the president of the assembly, who were there at the palace, and other people, other ministers, and I asked them to come to my office. Then we studied the constitution and began to think about the possibility of my resignation. I said to the group: "I may resign, but only if four conditions are met." The first one was to respect the physical safety of all the people and the government. The second one: respect for the constitution, meaning that if I resigned I would have to do so before the National Assembly and the vice-president would have to assume the presidency of the Republic until new elections were called. The third condition was that I be able to address the country live. The fourth one was that all the officials of my government should accompany me along with those guys who were my bodyguards for years. I knew that they wouldn't accept, because that would be a shock troop that I would have within my reach.

Then the emissaries—General Arturo Sucre, minister of infrastructure, and General Rosendo—went to Fort Tiuna. They talked to the conspirators and came back saying that, yes, they accepted the conditions.

I had authorized General Rincón, who had been with me the whole evening and night, to go to Fort Tiuna to find out what those people really wanted. In the middle of these events he called me and said: "President, they're demanding your resignation and they're putting pressure on me to resign as well. But I've said that I'll follow whatever decision you make." Then I told him: "Look, Lucas, Rosendo and Hurtado have arrived and they've told me that they accept the conditions that I am demanding for my resignation. Tell them that, yes, I will resign." I gave him the green light. He leaves saying what I told him. What he said was: "The president has accepted the demand for his resignation and so have I. My position is at the disposition of the high command." Therefore, I'm completely sure that he said what I had told him by phone.

What happened ten, twenty minutes later? He declares my resignation and leaves, but a few minutes later we receive word that they no longer accept the four conditions. I was almost certain that they were not going to accept; it was a way to stall for time. Next they demanded that I go there as a prisoner. If I refused they threatened to attack the palace. A few minutes after that, the situation changed.

And that was the end—I left as a prisoner. Lucas left. He took his family somewhere safe and on Saturday he returned to Fort Tiuna. He joined García Carneiro and the group of generals who were there reorganizing things. What can we accuse him of, then?

Has this information been released? Because as far as I know it hasn't reached outside Venezuela.

I explained that, I believe, to the special political commission of the National Assembly that investigated the events that took place during the April coup, when it interviewed me at the palace. I've said this before, to endorse him when I appointed him as minister of defense. He's a man who has been with me from the beginning of the government. He was the chief of the *Casa Militar*, he was a member of my ministry, he was commander of the army and then inspector of the Armed Force. And I appointed him minister of defense. Faced with a new political climate, which demands political dialogue, the most experienced man in my cabinet was José Vicente Rangel and this is why I promoted him from minister of defense to vice-president.

Can you summarize the lessons that you learned from the recent military coup d'état? You explained to me that in Fort Tiuna the commanders of the coup were in one building, and in another building farther away were the regiments. General García Carneiro—a man loyal to you—and his troops were in this building. You told me that the commanders had called him but he didn't want to report to them because he did not want to abandon his troops. Although, in the end, when he was told that they would go and talk to you in Miraflores he was convinced and left his troops without command. Some military chiefs involved in the coup took advantage of the situation to control the troops with manipulation and lies.

I've told you that I've always tried to respect the chain of command. The instructions from the commander-in-chief were always given through the higher ranks. Now, you can see what happened, the difficulties I had communicating with García Carneiro and other generals from the loyal military garrisons. I barely managed to talk to General Baduel[5] once and after that I lost contact. I couldn't reestablish it—they had cut the palace phone lines.

Well, from that we learned to establish more flexible communication mechanisms and direct contact from the commander-in-chief to the commanders of the operative units—those who have weapons in their hands and who command the men of the Armed Force.

It's not about disowning the highest ranks, it's just that in an internal or external conflict the high military commands may disappear for a series of reasons—they could be captured or physically eliminated. The top commander must have the capacity, the communication channels, in order never to lose something that is fundamental: the direct military command of the units of the army. That did not happen on April 11. The conspirators used this weakness to manipulate unit commanders, to neutralize other units, to deceive military chiefs who received information only from the conspirators, to disorient them, misinform them, confound them, lie to them, manipulate them. So this is a lesson: a much more direct contact with middle officers, the chiefs, the officers, and also the troops is needed.

Do you believe you can count on absolute majority support from those sectors?

Yes, absolutely. And I could prove it to you.

And how do the higher ranks see this?

Since it's not about lack of trust, but rather to be prepared for the worst, they shouldn't see it in a negative light. Although some jealousies may exist, I have worked to prevent any kind of jealousy from developing.

Don't you think that as the revolutionary process is radicalized it is more and more difficult to count on majority support from a group whose formation is very much influenced by the values of the ruling classes and that, therefore, is very susceptible to the campaign that the reactionary sectors launch against your government?

Yes, I think that's normal. I believe that this happens in any example anywhere in the world. Even if we apply the laws of physics to swimmers crossing the Orinoco River, there will be those who say "I can't go on" for physical reasons. The same thing happens in a group of mountain climbers; some will fall behind because of weakness or accidents. If this is what happens at a physical level, it's even more common in a complex process that is influenced not only by physical laws—which aren't even the most important—but also by culture, ideology, material, economics. There are people who go along with you through one phase—and we've lived it throughout this process, which for me, Marta, has lasted for almost twenty-five years, since I started to seriously organize small groups—but who later fall behind for any number of reasons. I have always tried to be thankful for that. I even thank those who are no longer with us because they helped at one stage. Their inability to move forward is no reason to condemn them. No, they just broke down, fell behind, or walked away for different reasons.

Many officers who were of great help before the insurrection didn't participate in the insurrection. But one can't forget their work. Of course, I'm not referring to the traitors but to those who fell behind for different reasons.

In prison, for example, there were people who had broken down or didn't want to continue. Many officers, my comrades, left prison and told me: "Look, *comandante*," or "Look, Hugo, I'm going home. I have my wife and children, I have to work to sustain them." I could never condemn them, quite the contrary.

I remember four guys who were with me once when we bought some bananas to feed ourselves; we ate bread, bananas and drank cola or coffee. We didn't have one cent. Everything we had was for the family far away, for our small children, our wives. One morning when I was sleeping in a hammock and the others were on mattresses, which weren't big enough for them all—we were in a walkway of a house belonging to a brave man who had let us stay; almost nobody dared to let me sleep in their house—I heard one of them crying. I came closer, thinking that he was dreaming, and when I asked him what was the matter, he answered: "My wife called me today. She's eating crackers and sardines." I then told him: "Well, you know that I'm the leader." "Yes." "I'm going to give you an order: tomorrow I don't want to see you here. Go to your wife, look for a job with someone who can pay you; I can't pay you anything." The guy didn't want to leave, but I ordered him to go.

He came back one day when I was already the president and worked with us for awhile. Later, he did his own thing, he took his own path. The majority went to look for something to do, somewhere to work; of course, they were young guys with wives and children. And then some of the radicals said, "They're traitors, they're weak." I think they're human—not everybody is like us, able to leave a loving wife and children; we don't care where we sleep; we have a dream. Perhaps we have a superior strength that pulls us through.

What I want to tell you is that I agree with you. I consider it normal that as the process demands more, it requires people with a higher conscience, capacity, strength, force. There are people who have their limits, and that's how far they go. One may be surprised negatively but also positively—sometimes one has the impression that some people can't surpass certain limits but they do indeed cross that line and even continue after that, and they keep moving ahead, leaving many others behind.

I believe that, in our case, there are more people who keep moving forward than those who fall behind. After February 4, the people advanced much further than I had previously anticipated. I remember how I felt in 1992 when we surrendered. What an embarrassment! "If we had only fought to the death," I thought, alone in my prison cell. Of course, I was isolated from reality. I didn't know the explosion of affection and emotion that the gesture of a group of officers had generated in the people. We had never imagined that. And what we saw at Las Malvinas the day before yesterday was a passion, a passion that had awakened in the majority of those people.[6] There are people who prove that they can go much further than you might think. Those who fall behind do so one by one, or in small groups. You'd have to be conscious of that. I mean, in the same way you were sensitive to the one you sent home, you should be able to detect when a person has reached his limit and make a decision about him before he breaks down, right?

Sometimes it's not easy. One needs to be very attentive, to work on developing that instinct. I do have good instincts and many times I regret not following them. I often pay attention to my strategic instinct, but sometimes I don't consider the small instinct regarding an individual. That happened to me before April 11; I will try to not let it happen again.

I've learned that an important group of young officers that has been leading the social front of the revolution has become more radical and demands more drastic measures against corruption. It asks for the acceleration of the rhythm of transformation. It doesn't understand your conciliatory attitude toward the generals involved in the coup. Am I right? How do you evaluate this attitude? How can one channel it? What can you expect from this group?

This sector or this phenomenon of radicalization of the military sectors has grown in favor of the revolutionary process; it has grown not only in number but also in intensity. You ask me how to confront this situation. What I try to do is exercise leadership. I have met with some of those who are upset because there are no military or civilian prisoners, and because the media continues doing what they're doing—disrespecting, fabricating, twisting the reality.

I try to make them understand that we're making an effort, as much as we can, to maintain the strategic option that we chose and that we are supported by a large majority of the country.

I am very aware that a process of deterioration of the current situation may result in the growth and increased power of these radicalized sectors. This is what some sectors of the opposition fail to consider. In the sense that they can remove Chávez, but they can't stop the process?

Yes, Chávez may go, but Chávez is not only Chávez. They tend to simplify the problem. The situation we are in has awakened very radical tendencies, feelings. I'm sure that no matter what happens to me, these radicalized sectors would keep going and new leadership would emerge. That, Marta, reassures me. Beyond my structural and political concerns and errors, I'm certain that this process is irreversible. This movement of change, of restructuring, of revolution, will not be stopped. Now, it is possible that its direction will change, that it will take another course.

I have said it publicly; it is not only a statement for you. No, I have said it, and many times it has been misrepresented as if I were launching a threat. No. I say it as a conclusion. Now, after what happened, I say it with even more conviction.

Here I can refer you back to the quote I mentioned earlier from John F. Kennedy when he said that if the revolutions in these countries were not peaceful, they'd be violent. That's when the Alliance for Progress was born. I read about that process in your book.[7]

Now, I'm convinced that if we were to fail in this effort of making profound political, economic, and social changes in this way, other paths will open, Marta, other ways will come. Perhaps violent ways, perhaps military ways, or perhaps civilian-military ways. But this process has assumed its own strength. I'd make an analogy to a river, a river you can dam but not detain. If you don't give it the possibility to flow, it will tear down the dam or find its own course, but it will always flow toward the sea.

CHAPTER FOUR

The Slow March toward an Alternative Economy

You have maintained that Venezuela cannot overcome the crisis it has suffered during the last several decades without a revolution. And, in order to accomplish the needed socioeconomic transformations it was first necessary to make important changes to the political-institutional apparatus. We have already analyzed some of the changes in this area—the major accomplishments as well as the obstacles along the way. Do you believe it is possible in the current situation to move the transformation of the socioeconomic structures forward, which you consider the key to the whole revolutionary process? There are those who suggest that the Bolívarian revolutionary process is not only unprecedented because it was able to reverse the April 11 coup and retake power in less than forty-eight hours, but also because there is a counterrevolution without a true revolution, in the sense of the socioeconomic transformation you talk about. Do you agree with that outlook, and if not, what have been the revolutionary steps that your government has taken in this area? What role does the government's strong support for cooperatives play in all this?

That is a provocative question, isn't it? Now that you mention all this, I remember what an African leader said: "The role of a revolution is to awaken the collective consciousness and get it on the road. The rest comes as a consequence." I do not totally agree, but

I do think this is roughly what we have done in our revolution. The awakening, the emotion, the desire to participate actively—these are things you didn't see before the revolution. In order to understand the progress we have made, you have to compare the situation today with that of ten years ago.

As soon as we started our government we set the course, the entire pedagogical, educational, participatory process in which the grand majority of the people comes to view the constitution as their constitution, though this is still a work in progress. I continue to insist that people read it, discuss it, analyze it, interpret it, love it.

In two hundred years of Venezuelan history, the people have never felt such a sense of ownership over a constitution. This is an unbelievably important step in the revolutionary process, and not only ideologically, but also in that we have been able to plant the Bolívarian concept into the soul of the people to such an extent that the oligarchy that used to call itself Bolívarian no longer wants to be associated with Bolívar. They had hijacked Bolívar and now he is back with the people. I'll say it again, this is an unbelievably significant step. It is something that is transcending our borders so that there are now Bolívarian movements in Spain, Germany, France, England, Senegal, Argentina, the USA, Canada, and so on.

The revindication of the essence of the nation is a revolutionary achievement that has practical implications in terms of sovereignty, self-esteem, goodwill, and solidarity. As Camus said in *The Rebel:* "I rebel and then we are." Here one recovers the "we are" where there was previously a domineering individualism, a failed sense of the common good. I have the image in my mind of February 4, 1992, in which I am standing with a rifle in one hand, looking through my binoculars, wondering where the people were. There was a failed sense of the collective then, but look at where we are ten years later. The world saw a people courageously defend their constitution, their imperfect revolution. There is a saying that the perfect is the enemy of the good.

That is what Petkoff says, I read it in one of the headlines of the newspaper *Tal cuál,* but Petkoff and the revolutionaries with him, when they were revolutionaries, were never capable of planting a uni-fying ideology in the soul of the masses. They did not reach the masses. Our revolution has reached the masses. There are people here who are willing to fight to the death to defend it. Even with doubts, imperfections, hunger, and that is why I don't agree with the saying: "love doesn't last when you are hungry." That saying is not applicable to a revolution, and certainly not here. The people who came out in defense of the revolution are hungry. Love lasts when you are hungry, though of course not forever.

It is not true that there is no revolution. We have a revolution here. There has been a change in the legal-political structure. Although it is still not perfect, it has flaws, it is threatened, it is just beginning, but nonetheless, a new structure is being born and we must protect it, strengthen it. Juridically, the new constitution is very strong, it has held up admirably and this has been recognized worldwide as a model democratic constitution. When we signed the Democratic Clause in Canada, we raised our hand and said "we sign this but we have to reserve our vote from representative democracy, we believe in participatory democracy." [1] And this has generated an international debate.

So, that is one factor. When we go to the heart of the matter, to the essence of the socioeconomic structure of the country, we have advanced very little, but the point is that the nature of this structure is very different from that of the legal-political structure. We were able to change the constitution—that is the legal structure. And in two years we were able to create a new political structure, but it still requires a lot of work. It would be delusional to think that in just two or three years we were going to be able to accomplish these profound changes in the socioeconomic system, especially taking into consideration that this is a peaceful process, strictly governed by the constitution.

If we had taken power through armed struggle, or even if not, if after the electoral victory, we had used violence, or a dictatorship, and began to detain people, to put the entire oligarchy in prison, to expro-priate their property, to nationalize banks, well, I don't know what would have happened. But we had a different strategy—legal-political transformation, which will later enable a calm economic transformation. If we had caused a major stir in both structures simultaneously, it might have been more than we could bear. We are talking about planned, preliminary phases. The first phase, the legal-political structure, is not finished but rather has passed the point of no return. That is how I see it, Marta. The constitution is going to hold up for years and years to come because to change even one little word, they are going to have to get permission from the people. Previously, political parties in Congress decided on constitutional amendments, but not anymore, now you must have a popular referendum, a public debate, and explain to the people why the amendment is necessary.

In terms of the socioeconomic phase, we have made little progress, but we are headed in the right direction. The coup is evidence that we are on the right track because the oligarchy, the counterrevolutionary forces, were counting on the failure of the revolutionary project, or their ability to push it off course, to neutralize it, or maybe they thought I would sell out, give in, retreat. Maybe the constitution didn't bother them so much, but in 2001 when we started passing the Laws of Empowerment, laws on land reform, fishing, banking, microfinance, hydrocarbons, and other laws through the National Assembly—obviously a very slow process—then the counterrevolutionary forces realized that the project would continue pressing forward, deepening the changes.

This explains their response. Why was one of the first counterrevolutionary decrees to void the Laws of Empowerment? Because they recognized the implications of those laws, and various sectors of the Right are trying to undermine the application of those laws through strikes, demonstrations, the coup, media pressure to change or void the laws through the National Assembly, or to get the Supreme Court to rule them unconstitutional.

The process is slow, complex, difficult, but the peasants are moving forward with the law. Are they going to take it away from them? Not easily, because the peasants are willing to fight for it, to defend it by any means necessary. I tell them to keep up the pressure, and we will keep up the pressure to demand that the laws are held in place. "Keep the pressure on the judges because you are the people and you have the power." Never before in Venezuela was there a law like this one, that allows community organizing, that gives priority to women in land allocation.

Can we clear something up? Are we talking about an empowerment law that enables the executive branch to write and pass laws, or are we talking about various empowerment laws?

Cabinet level ministers write a law, the president approves it, the National Assembly is notified, and it becomes law. That is how the budget law was passed, but there are still a whole series of social laws pending. The truth is it is one empowerment law, but we call all the laws passed through this process empowerment laws.

These laws are truly revolutionary, Marta, not as radical as some would like, but one has to find at least a minimal consensus without compromising the revolutionary principles. Often, this is a difficult process.

They say that in your campaign you promised that your government would not pay the external debt, yet you are servicing it. A lot of people on the left don't believe that a government can be considered revolutionary if it continues to pay its external debt when it could use the same money to solve so many basic material needs of its people. How do you respond?

I fully understand the concern, but I want to clarify that I never said that we were not going to pay the debt. There was a rumor to that effect, press commentary, et cetera. We did say that we would propose a scheme to restructure the external debt and in that respect we have not made progress, I have to admit it.

Why haven't you been able to make progress?

Well, because to make progress you need the goodwill of your creditors. You have to sit down with the bankers from the lending countries and establish the mechanisms for restructuring of the various components of the debt. That is one part of the problem. The other part is that we have had so many internal conflicts that we have not had time to thoroughly discuss the issue with our creditors.

Now, in terms of your question, I don't think that to be revolutionary a government must inevitably refuse to recognize agreements like its external debt. I do not believe that the debt is the key element in classifying a movement as revolutionary. It is about figuring out what is possible in the moment. As you have said, it is "the art of making possible tomorrow what appears impossible today."

If our government had refused to pay the external debt, there is no doubt that this would have saved us significant resources—eight or ten million dollars. We could have decided not to pay and instead used the money for development projects. If only it were that simple, everyone would support the decision. It would be a revolutionary, anti-neoliberal act.

But what would have happened if that had been our policy? That surely would have led to problems in a range of areas: foreign investments, for example, would certainly have been cut off. As you know, we have also acquired new debt to finance development projects like the Orinoco Dam, which we are building in Zulia; the contract that we signed not long ago to increase aluminum production with a major French company called Pechiney; the agreement with China to build a Chinese petroleum company; the Orimulsion plant[2] on the Orinoco, which will be able to produce four million tons of Orimulsion within five years, all of which the Chinese will buy; the harvesting of natural gas in the *Plataforma Deltana*. These investments total billions of dollars and they are all productive investments, but they also represent debts that the state has taken on. All these companies obtain credit from private institutions, sometimes public lenders, and they are investing it here.

If we had stopped paying the debt, saving those resources for social and economic investment, in all probability not one of those projects I just mentioned would have come to fruition. Any major international corporation—whether gas, oil, mining, timber, what-

Chávez returns to Miraflores Palace after being rescued
from Orchid Island, April 13, 2002

Chávez's return to Miraflores, April 14, 2002

Palace Guard celebrates arrival of Chávez, April 14, 2002

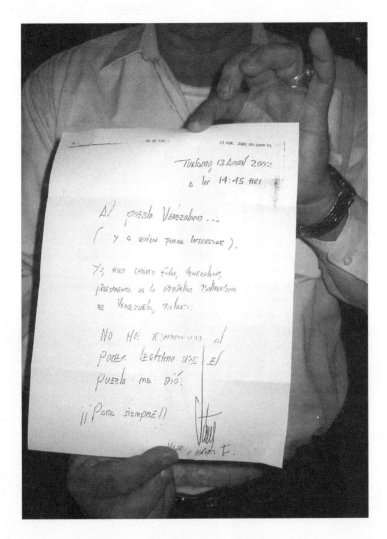

Note Chávez wrote from Turiamo declaring that he
had not resigned, April 13, 2002

Chávez arrives back from captivity , Miraflores, April 14, 2002

Minister of Defense, José Vicente Rangel arrives
at Miraflores, April 13, 2002.

Celebrating Chávez's return to Miraflores, April 14, 2002

Chávez with Attorney General Isaac Rodriguez (r), and then-
President of the National Assembly, William Lara (c), in the Salon
Ayachucho, Miraflores, April 14, 2002

Chávez and then-Vice President Disosdado
Cabello, Miraflores, April 14, 2002

Chávez presenting his radio program, February 1, 2004

April 25, 2004

ever—that goes to a bank to request a loan is going to have to tell the bank where they plan to invest the money. Then: "Oh no, but Venezuela doesn't service their debt! How could we lend you money to invest in a country like that?" None of those important projects would have been possible. We need to ask ourselves, given our modest place in the world and variables as overwhelming as the international financial system, how to best confront our reality.

Now, what do I have to say to the revolutionaries you referred to: first, all criticism is welcome. But, this is about trying to balance out the pros and the cons. Over the last several years we have dealt with a rapid political transformation of the country—internal and external disturbances related to OPEC, petroleum, conspiracies, the economy, society, the constitutional assembly, elections, more elections—with all this on our plate, if we had added one more major factor like the external debt to the complex hurricane, to put it one way, we would have run the risk of not being able to stay on top of the wave we have been riding.

Now, maybe if you told me that the global context, or at least the regional context began to change, and that a large group of countries began to move toward a position that allowed us more strength and flexibility, things would be different. If a political leadership rose up willing to face the risk together and explain their common decision to the world, to organize an OHIC, if you will allow me to invent a name here—Organization of Highly Indebted Countries, that ought to include Mexico, Argentina, Brazil, Venezuela, et cetera—then we could sit down together, five or six presidents, and tell the world that we are calling a meeting with the owners of banks A, B, C, D because between us we owe them something like one hundred billion dollars and we would tell them: "OK, gentlemen, we have made a decision in the name of our hundred or two hundred million citizens who elected us to govern them, to represent their interests. We want to pay the debt, but not as it is. We demand a change in the system of payment." Under conditions like those I have just laid out, with a more favorable balance of power, we might be able to accomplish something.

We could decisively, clearly say that we will not pay the debt, but I prefer a conciliatory path. So what are the available conciliatory paths? Well, there are plenty actually. One is called the International Humanitarian Fund: we sign an agreement saying that we legitimately owe x percent of the debt but we have already paid it three times over and we are still in debt. It is eternal, as Fidel has said, so we put the money in a fund that a UN-appointed board can administer to fight poverty in our own countries and in neighboring countries.

Another option would be to pay the debt but over a longer time-frame with a grace period of several years, given certain conditions. That is what we do here with the poor—we give them credit, but it is clearly established that no one should pay more than thirty per-cent of their family's monthly income to service their debt. If you earn one hundred dollars a month, you are not going to repay more than thirty. We do this to protect these people. There are thousands of other special programs we could develop that would produce resources for all, and these would also be valid conciliatory steps.

You know, we discussed a lot of these details not long ago in a meeting of presidents from several countries. One South American president stood up and clearly articulated his position: "Well, how is it that developed countries, or banks, or the IMF, or the World Bank can lend us money, for example, to build highways, and that gets incorpo-rated into our total outstanding debt, when at the same time the same financial institutions authorize loans for development projects in developed countries and that is not debt? The money is processed as development aid, or they pay back one part of it and another part they don't because it is aid for their people. Yet for the poor countries they pile on the debt with high interest rates." After that gentleman finished, I raised my hand and said: "Do you know why they do that to us? Because we do not have the courage to stand up for ourselves; it is our fault for not cutting out the whining and making the tough polit-ical decisions in the name of our people. Or, let's leave this meeting with the commitment to call a referendum in every country to see what our people want and then in a few months we can get together again with the results of those referendums, guided by our people's will, then we could begin to change the world. But we just keep talking, taking a few pictures and never making the tough decisions. We don't dare to defy the world. And as long as we fail to do so as a group we are not going to be able to develop as individual countries."

That is what the model for integration that I proposed is all about, the ALBA [Bolivarian Alliance of the Americas] as we call it. We are going to integrate with an eye toward solving the problems we have in common—housing is one of them. We are going to see how we can solve that problem in all our countries. Together we can do much more than any one can do alone.

Poverty, unemployment, the debt—we are going to figure out how to come together and tell the world: here we are, we have a common problem, and here is how we want to work on solving it. But if we all go it alone, we will not accomplish anything.

A few months ago, another South American president said that Argentina followed the neoliberal model to the letter, that it was the country that most closely followed that economic model. And now during its crisis, the IMF hung Argentina out to dry because apparently it isn't as important geostrategically as some other countries. But if we all took responsibility for Argentina's crisis, if we had a convention, just as in a war—if they attack one of us, they attack us all; that is what Bolívar put forward when he talked about just one army; if the *Santa Alianza* comes back to attack Ecuador, it is a war against all of us, not just against Ecuador. If we had applied that approach during the Falkland Island war, for example, the British never would have retaken those Argentine islands.

Now, there are plenty of factors that need to be thoroughly discussed before we develop a model for integration that will successfully address problems like the debt. As long as we fail to achieve this integration, we all have to go it alone through troubled waters. It isn't that we are scared to do it, it is about the viability of political decisions that can do much more to change the status quo.

I understand that you have produced a six-year economic development plan ...?

In effect, we have an economic development plan for 2001–2007, which was developed at the national level to strategically guide the country's economic development. Giordani directed a team of people, in consultation with many others including state governors, that developed the plan. After the cabinet ministers approved it, we sent it to the National Assembly, as the constitution requires, where it was debated for several months and finally approved.

How compatible is this plan with the process of decentralization?

Well, there is a contradiction there, and we have found the only possible solution allowed by our constitution, or at least one of the only solutions—planning through democratic, participatory, public debate.

We have been accused of being "enemies of decentralization," but really we are only opposed to decentralization that disintegrates the country's unity. One of the five strategic axes of the national development project is precisely deconcentrated decentralization. That is, we add the term "deconcentrated" to the concept of decentralization in the federalist model.

Why the term "deconcentrated"?

Because a central element of our decentralization plan is the deconcentration of political, economic, and social power. Really, the old, neoliberal style of decentralization created power centers within state governments. Governors became local *caudillos*, with total control at the regional level, at the same time as community participation from below was cut out of the picture. They understood decentralization but up to a point, up to the point where the communities actually started to get a share of the power and at that point they didn't decentralize anything.

Neoliberal policy proponents, just as their "invisible hand" in the economic market purports to magically solve problems of inequality and distribution of wealth, would have us believe that their brand of decentralization will take regional differences and automatically regulate the distribution of power. That will never happen their way.

I understand that there have been some experiments in various parts of the world with what have been called solidarity funds, where a certain share of the resources from the wealthiest state and municipal governments are directed toward poorer state and municipal governments in the same country...

Well, our constitution allows for that kind of fund. The idea is that the Council to the Federal Government would have an inter-territorial decentralization fund whose objective is to play the role that you just mentioned—a sort of voltage regulator, a homogenizer, that allows us to direct the most help possible to the regions that are most depressed economically.

However, the funds that we have created, the FIDES [Intergovernmental Fund for Decentralization], and the LAES [Special Economic Allocations Law for distribution of income from petroleum sales], favor the regions that are more developed, not the ones that are underdeveloped.

But in this area we have been moving forward slowly. We really ought to already have a new law of the Council to the Federal Government, which the vice-president should preside over that develops a compensatory fund to helps the most depressed states so as to balance out the regions across the country. With the current national government mechanisms, all we can do is concentrate the energy of our ministers on the most depressed regions, give special attention to states like Delta Amacuro, Apure, Trujillo, and Sucre, where poverty rates are much higher than in the rest of the country.

We have a national economic plan and that is why at the last meeting of the governors and mayors, I insisted on this plan. We can't move forward with an isolated plan for one state that fails to consider the development of the country as a whole.

Yesterday, I made it clear that we are only one government with various levels, divisions. The country should have only one government, and what unifies us, among other things (for some of us friendship and ideology are unifying factors, but that is not the most important thing now) is the plan that the National Assembly passed, a plan for the entire country. There are lots of governors and mayors, even some of ours, who have failed to grasp the strategic orientation of the plan, who are held back by inertia, etc.

Moving on to another topic, you have said that the Bolívarian revolutionary process is an alternative to neoliberalism. According to what you have said, it is an "anti-neoliberal revolutionary project," a "humanist, self-governing, fundamentally endogenous economic model that is not isolationist, and that is able to satisfy its people's basic needs,[3] but where human development is more important than economic development."[4] Does this mean that you believe it is possible to reform capitalism, to humanize it?

Capitalism as such, as an isolated economic system decontextualized from the political, social, and ideological—pure capitalism—is impossible to humanize.

When I met with [Istvan] Meszaros, the Hungarian Marxist economist, I invited him to criticize our work. He responded: "I don't have any criticisms, you are in a stage of transition and it is not something unique to Venezuela. It is impossible for a single country to try to launch an alternative model on its own, you will only go so far, it would be like when Napoleon tried invading Russia."

So this falls within what you were suggesting in your question. We are not talking about politics as the art of what is possible today, but rather as the art of making possible tomorrow what today appears impossible. Is it possible for Venezuela to transcend this moment, where the capitalist model has roots down into the very marrow, not only in Venezuela, but also in the whole world, especially surrounding us here in Latin America, in the countries on whom we are interdependent like Colombia, Brazil, and the United States?

But you asked me if it is possible to humanize capitalism. My answer is that in its most pure state—a vicious, wild capitalism as Pope John Paul II has called it—it is not possible to humanize it.

But in the case of Venezuela, with a government like this one, with a constitution like ours, with a people who have awakened like ours have, with a balance of power like the one we have, it is indeed possible to humanize capitalism. In these three years we have made progress. We are stuck in a capitalist system, we have not changed it, it would be dishonest to suggest otherwise, but, Marta, we have cut infant malnutrition by 10 percent, we have cut infant mortality dramatically by administering Cuban-made Hepatitis B vaccinations to all children. We have allocated much more money to education—from less than 3 percent to more than 6 percent of the budget; access to potable water has dramatically increased. These are a few humanist changes within the capitalist model. Of course all this is part of a transition phase.

I believe that the globalized world presents enormous challenges to revolutionary processes, and until now there has not been any revolutionary movement that can say it has developed a viable alternative to the current social order. Therefore, it does not strike me as odd that you put forward the need to invent a new economic strategy, recalling what Simón Rodríguez said: "Either we invent or we fail."

Marta, it would be awfully audacious of me to have my own definition when I see established intellectuals like Meszaros who are studying the issue. For our part, we are trying to move slowly but surely toward an economic alternative to dehumanized capitalism.

CHAPTER FIVE

A Sovereign and Independent International Policy

You are aware that excessive dependence on the United States would lead to a dangerous contradiction between Venezuela's revolutionary process and the neoliberal model that the United States seeks to impose on the entire region. With the vision of moving toward a multipolar world, you have been creating and strengthening relationships with other major players in the international political scene. Several of them, including China and Russia, are providing economic and political aid. You also have good relations with Canada, Brazil, and Mexico. You could say that you have been on the offensive in terms of international relations. You have initiated South American and Caribbean regional integration projects; you have prioritized relations with members of OPEC and worked with them to fix the price of oil at between twenty-two and twenty-eight dollars per barrel, an idea which the majority of developed countries have warmly received. At the same time, you have tightened relations with Cuba and other groups of developing nations like the Group of 15 in South-South cooperation and the Group of 77, which brings together more than 120 developing nations, and you were elected president of both of those two groups of nations. You also established a commitment to supply eleven countries in Central America and the Caribbean with preferred customer rates for petroleum, as a gesture of cooperation and goodwill.

And, in a convention with Cuba, you committed to supply that island with up to 53 million barrels of crude oil under a special payment plan and to cooperate in the recuperation of the Cienfuegos refinery. For its part, Cuba has committed to provide Venezuela with a series of services: medical services and products; generic medicines; technical support in the agricultural, tourist, and sports industries. On the other side of Venezuela, in the Southern Cone, you have sought to ally yourself with Brazil in opposition to the FTAA and to become a member of Mercosur. All this suggests that you, following Bolívar, understand perfectly that without some sort of integration there will be no future for our countries. Therefore, in response to the FTAA, you are proposing another kind of integration, the Bolívarian Alliance of the Americas (ALBA). What will this integration process consist of? Have you made progress in developing it concretely? What countries would support it?

It is about trying to reinitiate Bolívar's original idea—which of course was not only his idea, but others' as well—that he put forward at the Congress of Panama, the idea of forming a League of Nations: a union of republics.

In his letter from Jamaica in 1815, the Liberator was arguing for the need to form one strong, united country in the new world. But it was at the Congress of Panama where he developed the idea through political initiatives, after fourteen years of war and having liberated five countries from colonial Spain. So he proposed the League of Nations; a League of Republics, with one unified army. He even went so far as to propose the number of troops that each republic should contribute, based on its size—to New Granada, now Colombia, and to Mexico he assigned particularly important roles, but to Central America, less so. He already respected the differences between the republics that were still in their formative stages. But the idea was to have one unified army and navy, and a single economic model.

He talked about the idea of forming one political body to negotiate and represent the region to the rest of the world. At that time, Bolívar envisioned a multipolar world. And he did everything in his power to ensure that South America, including Central America and the Caribbean, would be one of those powerful poles.

We are trying to go back to this idea. That is where we came up with the idea for the ALBA. We would have to reexamine those historic documents, reconsider the whole concept. Bolívar ran into a lot of problems with the United States. He had serious differences with them. Once, he detained two North American frigates here in the Orinoco River, because they were carrying a shipment of arms to the Spanish. He said: "What brothers are these that fail to recognize our independence even after Europe has done so?"

Another time, certainly as a result of these tensions, he wrote in one of his prophetic letters: "The United States of North America seems destined by providence to plague [Latin] America with misery in the name of liberty." That was in 1824–25. Incredible how well he understood what was coming! Who knows how many other letters he wrote on these issues which have yet to be discovered. A lot of Bolívar's letters were lost—burned or lost at sea.

He wasn't only right to have doubts about the future actions of that great nation that was still in its consolidation process, but he also had apprehensions about Europe, the *Santa Alianza* that was threatening to retake the South American colonies. To be able to face any external political threat, it was necessary to develop this unified political body.

To do something new, we would have to begin by recognizing the failures of the neoliberal capitalist models of integration put forward during the twentieth century—models based on integration from above, of elites. That is why we proposed the ALBA.

You asked me if I had further developed that idea. No, I think that as a country and as the proponent of the idea, it is our responsibility to move the idea forward through contacts with all the alternative movements in the continent and throughout the world: the World Social Forum, for example; alternative social movements in each country. We should figure out how to move forward and further develop the idea of integration.

I put forward a few strategic elements.

One of the first things I put forward is the need to collaborate with the cavalry in front. What do I mean by that? You know that in war the cavalry is in front. Who has ever seen the cavalry as the rear guard? It is always the artillery that is the rear guard: the big heavy cannons that shoot from long distance. I buy my artillery with the economy; the cavalry with politics. So, as a result of the neoliberal model, we have the equation backwards: the horses are in the rear and the big or small cannons are in the front. We have to invert it. We have to retake politics. It requires that statesmen, politicians with a grand vision, begin making the decisions.

I am convinced of the need to move toward true integration, not just poetry and words. Economic integration beyond the typical tit-for-tat "I will buy that from you if you buy this from me," beyond tariffs and free trade zones. Who does all that help? More than anyone it helps the transnational companies, the local elites that can do a bit more business, but what happens to the people, to the real chains of production?

Look, we could negotiate an interesting agreement with Colombia. For example: Venezuela produces high-quality aluminum in Guyana and we export a lot of it as a primary material to Europe and the United States. For its part, Colombia has developed much more than we have their underwater aluminum processing plants, but Colombia buys its aluminum from Europe or other countries. How great would it be if Venezuela and Colombia formed a production chain that would allow the two countries together to produce our joint capacity of aluminum and its derivatives for sale on the world market! That is the kind of integration I am talking about.

Another idea I have is to form a South American Petroleum company—PetroAmerica—and why not also include Mexico? Venezuela has some of the largest oil reserves in the world. Colombia produces some seven hundred thousand barrels per day in spite of its internal political violence that impedes the exploration and harvesting of much of its potential reserves. Ecuador also has oil, but more than anything, natural gas, and the same with Peru. Bolivia mainly has natural gas. The five countries liberated by

Bolívar are energy rich: they have gas and oil. Add to them Brazil, which isn't a petroleum exporting country per se, but does have some oil and gas that it produces for internal consumption. Mexico is right up there and it also produces oil; Trinidad and Tobago, which are right next to us, are major producers of liquid gas. Why don't we form a PetroAmerica, a sort of OPEC right here in the region? But here comes the problem with the cavalry: where are the horses? Who makes the decision?

We have put the idea out there and up until now the only country that has responded is Brazil. Together with Brazil we are drawing up the documents and arranging the meetings, but we still haven't heard from any of the other countries in the region.

We also have projects using wood pulp for making paper. Venezuela imports the pulp, as does Colombia. But right here we have six hundred hectares of Caribbean pine that could be used to produce all the pulp we need between the two countries. We have to try to build a plant for producing wood pulp and making paper.

We have rivers, rivers that flood with the strength of nature. But we are missing the ability to control the rivers because we still haven't built canals and dams and so forth. We have so much natural wealth. For example, the Rio Meta that passes through both Colombia and Venezuela and is source of the Orinoco. On both sides of the border along that river, there is a huge savanna with enormous potential for cattle ranching.

What massive projects we ought to be able to develop together! But we are missing the beginning stages, the development of a model for integration.

On several occasions we have proposed a meeting of the heads of state to the Andean community, just to talk politics. The idea was approved in Cartagena in 1999, but the meeting was sabotaged. I guess it is not in some people's interests for the presidents of South America to talk about political integration. I proposed that we not talk about technical aspects, formal documents, chancellors, or free trade, just politics. It did not happen. That first year it didn't happen because we really lacked coordination. I won't say it was sabotaged that time, but in the second year they did sabotage the meeting. In Lima we kept insisting that we had not fulfilled our agreement and I proposed a new date; we had agreed to pick a date, but we had never agreed to one. I proposed December 9 and 10, in honor of Field Marshal Sucre and the Battle of Ayacucho, in Cumaná, Sucre's birthplace in Venezuela.

Once the idea was approved, we began to work on a document on future political integration for the summit. And what happened? We were a few months away from the meeting and we had already had several rounds of chancellors' and vice-chancellors' meetings, but then strange things started to happen in South America. First, I went to Bolivia for an official two-day visit and there was a popular protest to support me. Marta, that really surprised me but it was the first protest of its kind, a strong demonstration of popular support in another country. That was in 2000. There was a bit of discomfort in the government because of the protests, but of course they did not directly raise the issue. I left Bolivia and we headed to Brazil. Then, a few days later, rumors started circulating saying that I had met in secret with two indigenous leaders, including a Mr. Quispe. And that I was financing the occupation of highways in the coca producing regions of Bolivia. A few weeks later several people had been killed and they had to declare a state of siege, and well, it was all my fault because I had gone there, inflamed the country, met with Quispe, sent money, maybe even arms. . . . Kind of like what happened here with the Caracazo: twenty days earlier, Fidel Castro had been here for the so-called coronation of Carlos Andrés Pérez, and you know what they told us military officers, that the *Caracazo* was Fidel Castro's fault because he had come and left two hundred Cubans in the hills around Caracas and they were the ones who started all the trouble.

Well, so what happened in Bolivia was that Banzer [the former president], may he rest in peace, said that he would not come to the summit because I was causing problems. In Ecuador, a few weeks before the summit, a rumor got started that I was supporting Lucio Gutiérrez and other members of the military with arms and money to plan a military coup against Novoa. Novoa told me he was not coming. Paniagua, then president of Peru, said that he could not leave his country, but in his place he always sent Pérez de Cuéllar. They said that he couldn't come either because they had information that Vladimir Montesinos was in hiding in Venezuela. What a fuss they made. Pastrana, from Colombia, had said that he would come, in spite of the rumors circulating about our support for the guerrillas in his country, but only if the others all came. So there you have it, we had to suspend the meeting.

That same year there was an OPEC summit. I remember that on December 17, 2000, the ambassadors from all our countries were gathered in the National Pantheon. There, one almost never speaks, but I decided to say a few words: "This year father liberator, in front of your ashes we say it: your America is so divided that it is easier to bring together the heads of state from OPEC that crossed oceans and deserts to get here than it is to bring together the presidents of the countries you liberated." I left it at that.

And well, I have become fastidious because I have been trying to move things forward at each of our meetings, complaining that they have not fulfilled their promises, and I will continue to do so; it is crucial that we take up the issue of political integration.

You asked me which countries would support the initiative. I think that at this time no other country in South America would support it. Only Fidel told me I could count on Cuba.

Some heads of state, especially from the eastern Caribbean, who were in the meeting expressed their interest. But, I will say it again: those of us who proposed the idea have not done enough to develop it. We will have to work really hard on this one because it seems to me that it is a real alternative.

I am sure that the FTAA [Free Trade Area of the Americas] is not the way, it is not the way. So we have to figure out what is another way. I think Bolívar can help us out on this one.

What do you think of the possibility of organizing a plebiscite against the FTAA or a referendum, more than just a legal mechanism, like what they did in Brazil with the external debt? Because in the end it is about elevating the people's level of political consciousness.

That ought to be carried out through legal, constitutional mechanisms. We have the advantage that the Bolívarian constitution anticipates that before any major, transcendental national issue, the president is able to convoke a national referendum to consult the people, so as a constitutional mechanism it has more weight. But, yes I agree with you, before any national referendum it is necessary to have the debates, the movements, the forums, the workshops, and so forth.

And that the people be able to relate the issue of the FTAA to their daily life; I mean, a house-by-house popular education project. One of the things I like about the consultations is that they allow you to assign responsibilities to a lot of different people, especially to young people who in Latin America—not necessarily in Venezuela though—want to be involved, but there is never room for them. They don't want militant politics, or to be in a party, but they are prepared to take up concrete responsibilities as long as they feel useful. Imagine students going to poor areas to explain to people the consequences of the FTAA, the clash it represents with the Bolívarian ALBA and with what you are trying to do here. It could even transform itself into a solidarity campaign with Venezuela.

It is a great idea. A few days ago we were discussing the issue of political parties and that would be an unbelievably important task that many social sectors and political parties that support our process could take on; we would have to raise the issue like a flag. Until now it has not been done. We would have to do much more to develop the idea of the FTAA using the ideas that I have put forward in lectures and meetings with political leaders.

As I told you, I have put forward the idea of creating PetroAmerica, with the complementary economies; the integration of universities; cultural integration; the development of border areas. There is a whole series of elements, including some ideas about the integration model that are moving forward, but so slowly it is as though

they are on crutches. They could be useful—technical projects of
the CEPAL [Latin American Economic Commission], the ALADI
[Association for Latin American Integration], and the SELA [Latin
American Economic System]. There are institutions that have elab-
orated integration proposals that could go over really well. Neoliberalism did almost all of them in.

We South American presidents ought to give SELA and
ALADI and CEPAL a mandate, so that the political leaders begin
to deal with these crucial issues instead of the technicians, to
develop a realistic long-term, concrete integration plan. We could
have a commission look into it. We have the technicians to elabo-
rate the detailed proposals on integration. When you need time,
you make it, political will is what is preventing us from unleashing
the cavalry. I hope that, given the ways in which the political reali-
ties in several countries on the continent are in the process of
changing, these proposals will come to have more support at the
presidential level. Until then, we will have to focus our work on
social groups, political parties, so that these groups can increase
the pressure from below and develop their own movements.

Weren't you going to integrate with Mercosur?

Marta, within a week of my election I was in Brasilia and I said:
"Venezuela wants to integrate with Mercosur." President Cardoso
immediately gave instructions to his team to help make that happen.
But this generated a negative response from the Andean community,
as if Venezuela wants to destroy the community of Andean nations
and enter Mercosur. We cleared it up during a trip to Bogotá a few
months later—that we had proposed Venezuela's entry into Mercosur as a way to accelerate the union of the two South American
blocs. After lots of meetings, we agreed that we were going to support the alliance of the two blocs; but we have always said that if that
alliance does not move forward at a decent pace, especially with the
pressure we are under from the FTAA, Venezuela will continue to
insist on its incorporation into Mercosur.[1]

We are familiar with your position with regard to the events of September 11, 2001, in the United States and the war on terrorism that the U.S. government has been waging since then. Nonetheless, we would like for you to explain a bit about this crucial issue in terms of the global revolutionary movement. What do you consider to be terrorist activities? Do you consider the U.S. wars in Iraq and Afghanistan, or the Israeli aggression against the Palestinian people, to be state-sponsored terrorism?

Look, our position is quite similar to what China and Russia have put forward. France has also put forward ideas that are quite similar to ours. Of course we are not opposed to the war on terrorism; who could be opposed? But first, we say—what I said before that generated such a negative reaction from Washington—that you cannot fight terrorism with more terrorism. And I am not the only one to have said this. Javier Pérez de Cuéllar, Kofi Annan, the Pope, and Fidel all said similar things at that time.

We are ready to fight against internal or external terrorism, wherever it may be, but we have said that we will continue to "respect the self-determination of peoples, national sovereignty, international law, UN conventions, and human rights." That is our position and it is extremely strong ethically, politically, and legally. If some people don't like it, they don't have to, but it is our position and of course we will stand by it firmly.

Unfortunately, the issue has been painted as either black or white; it has been managed really poorly. I remember, in the trip I took through Europe last year, when that was the hot topic, because September 11 was so recent. I talked with Tony Blair, despite the fact that we already knew the UK's position on that issue, and he suggested that we needed some sort of global alliance to fight against the causes of terrorism, not just against its effects, and I applauded the idea. So I proposed that the G77 and the G8 meet together to thoroughly analyze the problem. But that has not been possible.

Now, with regard to the hunting down of terrorists, well, we are going to go after them. They have asked for our cooperation and we have modestly done what we can: we have sent our police to investigate, to track a few people, some bank accounts, or information that could help fight terrorism. We have done all that and we will continue to do so. But, I repeat, when it comes to international law, human rights . . .

What do you have to say with respect to the tendency to associate terrorism with guerrilla movements?

Look, there are guerrilla or subversive movements that end up being little more than terrorist movements. If a subversive movement puts a bomb in the middle of a city and that bomb hurts innocent people—kids, students, a police officer who happens to be there on the corner—that is an act of terrorism. If I were a guerrilla, I would not agree with that act; I would avoid hurting the civilian population—hitting electricity pylons, for example imagine how many social and economic problems that can cause for the people. I think those are acts of terrorism.

But in a war, are they justified? I mean, what is the difference between guerrilla warfare and conventional warfare? Because the guerrilla . . .

In conventional war you do things like that and more. They have dropped atomic bombs on cities, for example, in the course of conventional war. But let's move on to guerrilla war. I think I mentioned this to you a few days ago, remembering some old readings from when I was younger, that a nonconventional war needs to win popular support and keep it. To win popular support, a guerrilla movement had better not be flying into towers, putting bombs in cities, actions that target the civilian population. These tactics even hurt the movement that uses them. Of course, throughout history war has included these tactics, but even so, even as a soldier, I think it is deplorable. If I were a guerrilla, I would be incapable of putting a bomb on a crowded street. How am I going to know who happens to be there the moment the bomb goes off? And what if four kids come humming along on their way home from school? What gives me the right to put a bomb there without knowing who is going to be in the way, and if they will be innocent people?

Because of the enormous respect I have for human life, I have handed myself in on two occasions—once here in the history museum on February 4, 1992, faced with the risk that an unarmed civilian population would suffer the effects of a violent confrontation here in Caracas. That was one of the main reasons that I gave up my weapons at that time. I could see the slums that surrounded the military museum and I knew that there would be a bombing followed by a land attack to circle us, and well, I could imagine all those people living there. I looked around and saw kids peeking out of their windows. . . . I saw those people and I said: "they are not to blame for any of this; they don't even know what is going on." And then, ten years later, back in Caracas, I was faced with a very different situation, but that could also have led to confrontation and death.

By the way, now that you are talking about turning yourself in, I have a message from a woman who knew that I was coming to interview you and she told me, "Please tell Chávez that the women of this country say not to step down ever again, because we know that his heart is so big that he doesn't want any deaths. If he steps down there will be many more deaths. Please, tell him not to step down, that many mothers are scared of what will happen if he does." You know, they even said they were willing to die and to see their children die if necessary to ensure that the process here can move forward.

Marta, that is a really powerful message for me. I know that a lot of people think like that, and I tell you this so that you will write it: "I surrendered on February 4, 1992, at around 10 A.M., and I surrendered ten years later on April 11, 2002, at around 3 A.M., but if it happens a third time, I am not sure that I will surrender, no matter what might happen to me. That is for you to tell to those worried mothers, and the young people, and to all the people who send me notes saying "Chávez, don't go again, don't do that to us again."

But, getting back to the issue of terrorism and guerrillas, I want to clear something up: in the case of Colombia, we have not called the Colombian guerrillas terrorists. Now, it is true that they plant bombs and so on, and that we consider those acts to be degenerate forms of war. But not even those acts lead us to classify this or that movement as terrorist, because we believe that it is not our place to do so. One must look for political solutions, dialogue, peace negotiations. If we call the Colombian guerrillas terrorists, we would be closing off the possibility that we could play a role as mediators—which is what we would like to do, if the various parties would like us to—to help move toward a peaceful resolution. What we do ask, not only of the guerrillas, but also of all the armed actors in the Colombian conflict, is that they do not use violence against civilian populations.

That is our position with respect to terrorism; basically, I insist on the concept of fighting against the causes of terrorism.

As the world is going about it—I have said it before—it is not viable. If the differences between rich and poor, between developed and underdeveloped, continue to grow, if every day there is more destitution, more hunger, more death, well, that is another kind of terrorism. There are all kinds of terrorism: hunger is one of them. And we must fight against this terrorism even more so than against other kinds of violent terrorism.

How great would it be if the world would realize this and if every day there were more good will to work toward human development, as the UN and the FAO [Food and Agriculture Organization] have asked us to do. The secretary general of the FAO said in Rome that instead of increasing, the aid developed countries give to poor countries has decreased. Development programs, or efforts against terrible diseases like AIDS, or malnutrition, have all decreased, especially with neoliberalism.

So, if we keep on this track, and every day the number of poor in Latin America, in the Caribbean, in Asia, in Africa is increasing, where will the world be headed? The world is headed for disaster, a terrorist collapse.

Don't you think, as the Egyptian economist Samir Amin says, instead of organizing a coalition against terrorism as the United States is doing, we would do better to organize a coalition against war and social injustice, that we could then try to stop future wars and also unmask all the efforts to paint all sorts of national liberation struggles, campaigns against poverty in the third world, and anti-globalization movements in the North, as terrorism?

I would be very much in agreement with that kind of a proposal. At various international summits, we have put forward the idea of creating an international humanitarian fund by reducing military expenditures. We have talked about this for a long time, but where is the political will to make it happen?

I would prefer, for example, that the nearly five billion dollars that Venezuela is going to pay this year—we have already paid half— could be invested not only for our people, but also for poorer people within our region. I am thinking of a special program that Venezuela would not be in charge of, a humanitarian fund for the production of food for malnourished children, for the poorest countries, like Haiti, for example, throughout the region; special programs to vaccinate against diseases . . . I am talking only about the case of Venezuela, but if a percentage of the Brazilian debt, of the Mexican, of the Argentine . . . could be directed in that way, I don't think it would derail the world economy. On the contrary, I believe that people with greater levels of development will have a greater capacity to incorporate themselves into a productive economy.

Last year at the Summit of the Americas in Canada [April 2001], we proposed to all the presidents of the continent, with the exception of Fidel, because, as you know, he was "democratically" excluded, that in light of the grave social crisis facing our region, we declare a social emergency in the continent. I asked that we do it right there in Canada. I put out the idea of naming a commission that would make a report within a year. You would not have to do any diagnostic study. It is a clearly visible reality: hunger, unemployment, poverty, and all that is destabilizing democracies; it is a political, economic, social, and a kind of terrorist destabilization. No one responded, not even to speak out against my proposal. How nice it would have been if someone got up and said: "I disagree with that proposal." "Ah, very good, tell me why, what do you propose instead?" But no …

The neoliberal model has done a lot of damage. It believes that opening markets and international investment are the solutions. Sometimes I feel indignant when I hear heads of state from Europe talking about how aid to Latin America should be conditioned on efforts to combat corruption there. And that we should decrease the size of our states; conditions that lack respect for our sovereignty, that are impossible.

And speaking of international relations, what can you tell me about what was reported in the newspaper El nacional *about the United States trying to open an office for transitional initiatives in Caracas?*

Before we take a position we are looking into what exactly that office would be all about, we have basically just heard about it through the press and I think anyone can understand why we have our doubts about the huge headlines of the opposition press. It could be journalistic manipulation to provoke a reaction from us, so we are moving forward nice and slow, very cautiously, so that we don't make our relationship with the United States any more complicated.

Therefore, we feel a bit indignant. We have requested that the U.S. government, through its embassy, clear up the situation. We are also looking for other sources of information. They have explained a few things, but not enough details. Let me read you what the newspaper *Últimas noticias*—one of the most objective ones here—wrote on Tuesday, July 23 [the day of this interview]: "Yesterday the U.S. Embassy in Caracas confirmed that the U.S. government is considering the possibility of opening a 'transitional initiatives office,' and stated that its objective would be to 'strengthen democracy.' The press attaché from the embassy, John Low, said that the initiative is being considered in Washington because of the complicated situation

Venezuela is experiencing. This is a proposal that has been under consideration for months, it is possible that it would go under our international programs for strengthening democratic institutions," Low confirmed. "If the office is opened, it will be a public process and it will work with the government, the opposition, NGOs, citizens. . . . " He explained that the office's name comes from the work carried out when it was first established to assist countries making the transition from communist regimes to democratic regimes.

How should we respond to that? First, we ought to watch it closely, pay attention calmly and patiently. We should investigate thoroughly. Up till now they have explained it as just a possibility. I can tell you that today I am going to assign Chancellor Chaderton the responsibility—and he has fulfilled it in the past—of making the U.S. government, through its embassy in Caracas, see that this sort of initiative would not help our efforts to decrease internal tensions, to look for alternative solutions for the country, which we have been making all attempts to do.

On the other hand, it is known that we are open to dialogue. We have worked with governments from all over the world, we have invited the Carter Center and the UN to visit us. We have said that anyone who is interested can come here as long as they respect our sovereignty and come with the intention of cooperating.

Now, why do I say what we have said to the U.S. government, that in our view and in light of the little information we have, that this office will not help? Because it would generate, as it already has begun to do in certain opposition sectors, the idea and the perception that the U.S. government is supporting them. It was that sense of security and support that led them to attempt the coup on April 11. During the months prior to the coup, when sectors of the opposition went to Washington, they were well received by the government there. On several occasions I explained to previous ambassadors and to the current one, and I also made it clear when I went to the United States, that I thought the warm reception the people who were conspiring here received in Washington was very risky because it could give them the impression, and other people, even our government the impression, that the United States was supporting and giving the green light to their conspiracies.

All this about the transitional office could have the same effect. And the worst part is that this is happening at a time when there are objective reasons to feel optimistic. There are some groups within the opposition that have come around to recognize the need to find solutions that are not violent, traumatic, extra-constitutional, and this could help isolate the most radical groups, the extreme right wing, and the counterrevolutionaries. That is where we are directing our efforts in terms of dialogue, to fix a few pressing issues through the cooperation of international leaders and organizations.

So, establishing an office like they are talking about doing, with the name and the history it has, could add fuel to the fire we are trying to put out.

That is as much as we can say up until now, today, July 23, 2002.

But if in the future this office is actually established, we will have to develop a more concrete position and bring the issue first of all before the country, our institutions—some representatives of the opposition have already come forward to applaud the idea, and of course many sectors have come out against it as well—and then to the international community.

On the other hand, there is already a transition in process. Venezuela has been in the midst of a transitional process for three years in terms of its political, social, and economic models, as indicated by the constitution. This is our transition. Now, if the U.S. government wants to have a greater presence in Venezuela to support it, which is the only transition I will recognize, then they are more than welcome. If the US government wants to send some advisors, some teams to help us with our micro-credit program for the poor, to build houses for the dispossessed, to help apply the law of the land, they are more than welcome. And they will continue to be welcome to help in that way, as will any other government.

If the U.S. government is interested in Venezuelan oil, the best way for them to continue getting it would be to support our government; we can assure them that they can count on our oil. It is in our mutual interests to maintain trade relations. Actually, destabilizing the country politically would only put their Venezuelan oil supply in jeopardy. Can you imagine what would happen if there were another coup attempt here, whether military or institutional, like some people are trying to organize? This country would be transformed into a war zone. If in Colombia there are zones affected by the guerrilla presence, if they sabotage the oil pipelines, what would happen here with a people and an army who see this government as their hope for the future?

I want you to know, Marta, we do not have any interest in complicating or damaging our relationship with the United States, much less in cutting it off. Nonetheless, we have always been firm and clear on the issue of sovereignty, independence, and we have put that forward not only to the United States but also to all the countries of the world.

CHAPTER SIX

The Middle Class, Communications Strategy, and Dialogue

In Chile, one of the primary causes of Allende's overthrow was that the Right developed extremely effect anti-Allende strategies—among them economic destabilization (capital flight) and political-social destabilization in which the media played an important role in isolating the radical popular sectors from any support in the middle class. Do you think that something similar is happening in Venezuela and that it would be important to the Bolívarian process to maintain the support of the middle class, intellectuals, and professionals who, in spite of their small numbers, are qualitatively important because their support could result in the development of countless supporters, trained in the skills necessary to meet the enormous economic and social challenges that the country faces? Do you think that you have had an appropriate strategy with regard to these sectors, which, according to my understanding, mostly oppose the revolutionary process? What would you have to do to regain their support? I have heard that you surround yourself with people who are loyal, that loyalty is very important for you. Often these people are very loyal, but not so efficient and they sort of form a ring around you that prevents other people from being able to collaborate in support of the process. On the other hand, there are those who maintain that there are lots of people from the middle class who want to help the needy popular sectors, that they do not like you but are willing to work on projects to improve the quality of life for the people. They feel there is no room for them, that they are being underutilized. What can be done to integrate those people?

I will not deny that there may be sectors—let's call them loyalists or *chavistas*— that have sectarian attitudes and tend to build walls that isolate the process and the government from important middle-class groups. But I do not think it is the primary characteristic of the government, or of the groups around me. If someone were to analyze the composition of the cabinets that have been in place over the course of my government, they would realize that the majority are not members of the MVR party.

We are aware of the need to integrate the diverse sectors of the revolutionary process. As I told you, before we were elected we were working with a document that we called our "strategic map."

That is how the MVR was born; the alliance with other parties, primarily those from the center, from the right, and other small groups were also incorporated. More than these alliances with political parties, we had the polynomial of power with the strategic goal of building alliances with sectors of civil society like the church, businesses, intellectuals, academics, professionals, and so forth. Since then, we have made every effort to keep those sectors together, but we have not been successful in this crucial area. Of course, it is like a game of chess; I have my pieces, I prepare my move in my head and then I go for it, but in front of me there is an extremely powerful adversary, with the capacity to influence these sectors, especially through control of the media, which has a huge impact on the middle class. That is where the impact of this bombardment, now going on for ten years, is felt. The demonization campaign began right after February 4, 1992, and instead of decreasing in intensity it has increased in intensity and focus on me, against our project, our attempts to form that wide base we call the polynomial of power and that is directed at the middle class, intellectuals (what some call "thinkers," a term that is quite . . .)

Pejorative for the rest of us?

Yes, because we all think. We have tried, on many occasions, to win the support of the middle class, of the intellectuals, but we have not been successful. Our adversaries' strategy has been more successful, and we have made mistakes.

But going back to what you mentioned about how I surround myself with people who are loyal, I think the criticism refers more to hard-line *chavistas*—as they are called—than to loyalists.

But at the end of the day I get criticized. They say that I have chosen my teams from too broad a base, and I think I have done that because of the idea of the polynomial of power. For example, in my first cabinet I had people like Alfredo Peña, who went on to become the mayor of greater Caracas and a fierce adversary of both the project and me. Why did he enter the government, whose error was it? It was mine. I appointed him minister of the Secretariat because he was a journalist, a man with many years of experience in TV, with lots of connections to groups within the middle class and I thought he would serve as a channel of communication, a connection with diverse sectors including the media.

If you look over other names, you may find some prestigious university professors, like Héctor Navarro, who was the director of graduate studies for years at the Central University. He served as minister of education for three years and then as minister of higher education. Through him, a lot of people that I did not know came into the government, including María Hanson, a very dynamic woman who was vice minister of education management. The Bolívarian schools project was their idea. María had been a member of the board of directors of the Venezuelan Confederated Association of University Professors and still had lots of contact with them. Carlos Lanz, an ex-guerrilla, a leftist and a writer, also worked in that ministry. They did something that had never been done before: they called it the *Consituyente Educativa* [educational constituent process]. They had hundreds of meetings in the schools with parents, representatives, teachers, and students to present the National Education Project (PEN). That is how they came up with the idea for the Bolívarian school project and other ideas that involved lots of educators.

If we continue analyzing that first cabinet you would find another gentleman, a writer and a planner: Jorge Giordani, who I mentioned earlier. He spent three years as the minister of planning and development.

Another example would be the ministry of the environment, directed by Elisa Osorio, a woman with an extremely strong academic background, a doctor who specialized in low-income health care. Of course we have also incorporated lots of people with environmental science training into this ministry.

So, over the course of these years, a range of teams formed in which a lot of "loyalists" participated. Perhaps that is not the best word to describe these people, but rather the sectarians. We still have people who are totally closed off to others and I want them to get over it.

But beyond just the government, in areas like the constitutional assembly there were tons of new faces. A lot of the new members of the National Assembly do not have long political histories. Many of them were academics, journalists, writers, singers, poets, etc. Really, the government was quite open at the beginning; it was not a government that came to power closing itself off to other sectors.

But when we began to realize that our adversaries were taking advantage of that openness to penetrate, infiltrate, and neutralize the process, push the process off course, then the natural tendency was to begin to close. And this has happened to me even with people like Luis Miquilena, who stood firm, who worked for so many years, extremely skilled politically, with diverse contacts; he was almost eighty years old and had a wide range of experience. But then we realized that he did not share our goals, the revolutionary strategy that drives us. So these kinds of people have started leaving, and it makes one think that it might be necessary to close off a bit. This closing off has been a recent phenomenon, a reaction to attempts to infiltrate the government.

In any case, I accept that we have had few successes with that plan or the program of the polynomial of power, and we should consider the reasons for that failure. Are we talking about our mistakes? I can't deny that the factor you raised in your question is relevant. But you also have to consider that before we took over the government, a lot of the best and brightest intellectuals had been cooperating with the oppressive regime in power. This is detailed in a book called *El antichavismo y la estupidez ilustrada,* by Nestor Francia, a good leftist Venezuelan journalist. In the book, he provides a quite interesting analysis about the attitudes of these sectors.

But I think the main factor, the most devastating, has been the media.

I have read an interesting document produced by a group of intellectuals, among them, Edgardo Lander: Un diálogo por la inclusión social y la profundización de la democracia, *published in May of 2002. It supports the process, but expresses criticisms. I think that the events of April 11 opened a lot of people's eyes and as a result there are now better conditions for dialogue with sectors of the middle class, especially with intellectuals. I understand you read the document and called a few of its authors to try and arrange a meeting with them.*

That is true. Those meetings are still pending, because it fell through on two previous dates, but I asked Vice President José Vicente Rangel to meet with them and he has done so. I have to see them. It is one of our failings that we have not been able to take advantage of the support available from some groups of intellectuals.

While we are talking about professionals, it surprises me that there are so few revolutionary foreigners who are working in support of the process here. I remember how many Chilean professionals went to support the Cuban process and the same thing happened in Nicaragua. Have the times changed, or is it that you have not been able to mobilize that support? Thinking about your communications strategy and the many problems you have recognized in it, there are excellent journalists in other countries that might be willing to support the project here.

Well, I think there are problems on both sides. First of all, there are our failures. But the media coverage of the process in general, and of me in particular, has had international ramifications.

If I were a left-wing intellectual from any Latin American country, observing this process from a distance, I would probably have my doubts [about] an army officer governing the country and moreover one who already attempted a coup. And add to that all the stories the media tells. For example, throughout South America we are often associated with the painted face group from Argentina [a fascist military group from Argentina]. I remember once when I was arriving in Buenos Aires, the first time I went, the headlines said: "The Venezuelan painted face has arrived." The Left and the sectors of the intellectuals were gone.

Now, you know the first person who broke out of that attitude was Fidel.

We were eager to work with social and political groups in Colombia, but it was hard, we were rejected because they associate us with the guerrilla, with the armed struggle. We went to El Salvador for the São Paulo Forum and there we met a lot of people, but many of them were thinking: "Careful, here comes the coup-mongering colonel."

I made every effort, I traveled the continent, I met a bunch of people in 1994–95 and I was able to make some important contacts, but all this hardly amounted to anything. It was not easy because of the prejudices, the lack of a support team, of resources, sometimes we couldn't even pay the phone bill and they cut us off. On more than one occasion we had to work in borrowed offices. Of course, we also made a mistake, we undervalued this aspect of the work and I am sure that affected us.

One time, I went to Mexico to talk with Cuauhtémoc Cárdenas, who had just been elected mayor of Mexico City, but we couldn't accomplish anything because the Mexican PRD party was one of the ones that had been most opposed to our integration to the São Paulo Forum back in El Salvador. I felt like I was in the Inquisition. They asked me to write a letter so that they could consider including us but we never sent the letter because the truth is I was getting the cold shoulder from them.

But the situation has changed dramatically since the April 11 coup. The coup attempt generated international sympathy for our process. For a lot of people, the reaction of the right wing, the coup attempt was proof that we are trying to bring about serious change here. At the same time, we have developed a deeper understanding of the importance of developing contacts and international support. You have seen the wealth of personalities, forums, workshops, seminars that are being held right here in Caracas.

Even though we have an international focus in the MVR and the Revolutionary Political Command, we still have lots of problems in terms of our international strategy. We could still really use a more dynamic chancellor of state who could move forward the government's efforts to develop an international support network.

There are lots of civil servants from the previous government still working in our embassies who do not fulfill their duties or, worse still, block or sabotage our efforts to establish contacts with sympathetic political groups, intellectuals who are sympathetic to this process.

One of our current challenges is to figure out how to advance and consolidate in those international arenas. And we need to figure out how to face the powerful opposition-controlled media, which continues to condemn us and slander our efforts.

One of the first things they did, for example, was publish pictures of cultural groups protesting because they had not received funding and that led some intellectuals to say that "Chávez does not care about culture, he denies funding to cultural activities." They use that strategy at every opportunity. But meanwhile they do not cover the real efforts we are making in the cultural arena. You saw the model schoolhouse in Puerto Cruz that is so different from the previous ones,[1] the kids with proper clothing for their traditional dances. Now they have a dance hall, a decent playground, room for studying and thinking. We have been building cultural centers in small communities, towns, poor neighborhoods. Some of them have computer rooms with free Internet access, or dance rooms, small theaters, all modern up-to-date equipment, with the support of our government and the guidance of local governments. The media totally ignores all this work supporting national culture.

It is also true that we have made a lot of mistakes in our communications strategy. I am a bit obsessed with our communications strategy and sometimes I am too hard on my team when we fail to predict things. For example, this morning I spoke with my father, the governor of the state of Barinas, and he told me, "Well, Hugo, yesterday we delivered fifty tractors," as part of a program that the national government developed with Brazil. Out there the agricultural equipment— tractors, reapers, planters—was totally destroyed and it had been ages since they had had any government support for medium and small-scale producers. So I asked my father, "Did you bring me a video, did you film the project?" Because the country does not know that we are delivering new, modern tractors to farmers.

So few know that we have had a successful housing plan that helped the middle and lower classes. Two years ago we had a project to assemble a low-cost vehicle and we had huge sales successes. Who does this success benefit—more than anyone else? The middle class. Again, through all this, we have made mistakes in our communications strategy: for a series of reasons we have not been able to get the intellectuals, professionals, and the whole country in general to realize that what we are doing helps a lot of people, in particular those sectors.

May I interrupt?

Of course, I tend to talk a lot…

During the Allende years we had the same problem in Chile. On the one hand, the opposition maneuvered to maintain control of the media. The Democratic Christian party agreed to support Allende on three conditions. One of them was that he would not touch the media— those that inform with disinformation—and the other two were that we would not touch the armed forces or the education system. When the government wanted to implement a more democratic education system with a social orientation, there was an incredible reaction from the right wing. On the other hand, the Left and progressives were used to the opposition media but didn't know how to create alternatives that could inform the people about what the government was really doing.

We are trying to put out two newspapers that cover the actions and initiatives that our government is taking and which the mainstream media ignores, or buries deep in the paper. A good paper would definitely have a positive impact on these sectors.

But, going back to the Venezuelan situation, I don't understand how it was possible to write a new constitution during the information age and not put in place procedures that allow for some control over opposition media. It seems to me that these companies are totally undemocratic, I mean, a press corps that is not objective, does not help the country, encourages destabilization, and supports the coup. I don't think I have been to any other country with such a libertarian approach to the press.

The term "truthful information" was inserted into the constitution. That was passed after considerable debate. The media and their political representatives couldn't block that phrase from being included. On the other hand, the Supreme Court issued a statement last year in which they upheld the constitutional principle of truthful information, affirming that the media are obligated to respect that constitutional principle. We are now working on a legal project—one of the things they have been trying to stop—called the Law of Media Content, which, once approved, will establish much more detailed norms and rules to develop that constitutional clause about truthful information.[2]

I mean, it is not that we have had a total absence of legal instruments for regulating the press; it is just that in the last three years, the media has gone beyond the pale.

Now, I was telling you about a dilemma that we have been trying to sort out: how to ensure that the press, TV, radio, and the people who direct them or use them stay within their constitutional, legal, and ethical limits.

We have tried to establish dialogue, to influence them through a range of procedures, but without a doubt we have not managed to do so. Lately, what has happened is that they have shown us they have no interest in moderation, in staying within their constitutional limits. They are putting up fierce resistance with the support of the international community, including the OAS.

We know there a lot of people who are complaining: "You have to be tougher on the media, you have to get them to fall in line." At this point I think the only path left open to us is coercion, in the judicial-legal sense. There is a telecommunications law that was passed in 2000 as one of the empowerment laws, and it establishes sanctions for the media. CONATEL (the National Telecomunications Council) has been administering fines and opening administrative procedures to determine lesser punishments in spite of the fact that there has been more than enough evidence to warrant harsher measures, and we have chosen not to apply them. But it is just as well that they know we have not renounced the possibility of taking more drastic measures.

I understand there has been a proliferation of community-based media throughout the country and that these can serve as important tools for making the truth known and for helping to organize these communities. What do you make of this phenomenon?

Community-based media is really important in restraining the distortion campaign of the privately controlled media. We cannot remain quiet in the face of the private media campaign to poison the people's outlook.

I know that there has been a popularly led boycott against the newspapers and TV channels that undermine the democratic system and that it has been so effective as to force the owners of the reactionary private media—El Nacional and El Universal and Globovision—to admit the massive decrease in their sales and ratings. For example, Miguel Salazar, the columnist for the weekly Quinto día, admitted that his paper's sales had decreased dramatically, a situation that he classified as "worrying" in light of the paper's historic sales. For its part, the channel Globovision had to admit its ratings during prime time dropped between three and five points over the last few weeks. I also understand that in addition to the media boycott, there has been an attempt to boycott products advertised on opposition media. The role that consumer organizations can play in confronting certain policies has always seemed really interesting to me. But since we don't have a lot of time, I prefer not to get caught up on this topic and would like you to talk about your Sunday program. Why don't you explain how the program Aló presidente *came about and what led you to develop the program in the ways you have.*

The idea developed at the beginning of our government, as a product of our communications weakness.

Was it your idea?

The idea came out of a team of three or four people that worked with me during the electoral campaign. We came up with the idea while evaluating our terrible communications deficiency. That was where we came up with the strategy of using me as a means for communicating with the people, given the weight I had—and it is hard for me to say it, but this is the truth—and my role in the process, especially at the beginning of our government.

We got started with a newspaper called *El Correo del Presidente.* It was a good paper but it fell apart.

Why did it fall apart?

Although it had a good design, a good message, it was too much the official government line, and we also had distribution and management problems. It lasted a few months and played an important role.

How big was its circulation?

I don't really remember, but it was around twenty thousand.

Ah, so was it a clandestine newspaper?

Almost.

It did not reach everyone . . .

No it did not. Then we had a live weekly TV program called *De Frente con el Presidente*, every Thursday night in a studio packed with people who asked questions or who called with their questions. It wasn't bad, but it got too heavy and we started losing our audience. I think the program's format was wrong, perhaps with a new format . . .But the idea is still valid; I have always liked the idea.

Then we came up with the idea for *Aló presidente* on Sundays. At that point I had two programs, one on Thursday and one on Sunday. Initially they were just radio programs that mainly consisted of an avalanche of phone calls. We tried to keep the questions and my answers short, especially my answers, because I have a tendency to go on and on in my answers. We always did it from the same place: the National Radio of Venezuela's headquarters that is located in a densely populated middle class part of Caracas.

It was on Sundays at 9 A.M. and sometimes it went until 2 in the afternoon. The format was based on phone calls; I insisted they let as many people as possible call in; there was no script. I arrived, sat down, and said, for example, "Good morning, today is Saint Barnabas Day, it is Sunday, it is raining and what else, are there any calls? And the program was developed in accordance with the topics our callers raised. They were almost always women calling in with problems. Some called with criticisms, but not too many because of the avalanche of calls that always followed defending the government and because of my tough answers.

The program lasted about five hours and halfway through we had what we called "the hour of lead"—it got everyone riled up and I quite liked it—it was pure hard copy, and tough attacks . . .

Who were you attacking?

We went after the opposition, the media, and so on. It was a program with a lot of energy. From the beginning lots of transmitters were getting on board, especially the regional ones. At one point we had a hundred transmitters broadcasting our signal, it was as though we had a national radio chain.

But what happened? Since we did every Sunday at the same place in a building that only had one exit, the lines of people with notes and letters, crying and waiting out front for me became untenable. When I got there around 9 A.M. people were already there, they came from all corners of the country and spent the night there waiting. The neighbors started to complain because there were no services set up for them. They were handling their bodily necessities all over the neighborhood. They slept in the doorways of houses on little makeshift mattresses. Well, that phenomenon was on the rise until we finally said, "No, we can't keep doing the program here, we have to change the locations."

Then we began doing it from a small studio in Miraflores, but there it was too isolated from the people, so it occurred to me that we should start doing it from different places all over the country. And so we have broadcast programs from Bird Island to La Sabana; we have traveled the entire country.[3]

We kept doing the program every Sunday and I brought a plane full of government ministers and journalists with me to each new location. But at a certain point, I will confess, as a result of my exhaustion from doing the show all day Sunday, getting back late that night and starting the week the next day, I decided to move the program to Saturday. I committed to spending at least a bit of each Sunday with my own family. But when we switched it to Saturday, the audience decreased significantly, because on Saturday people get up and go to the market and run other errands. The decrease in our audience was so sharp that the opposition began to exploit it, saying, "six million people have stopped listening to Chávez." And that was true because a lot of people had followed the program.

When we saw that, we met with a team of people—ministers and other state employees—to see what we should do because we could not abandon the communications front to the opposition: José Vicente Rangel, his wife Anita, who knows a lot about these issues; Diosdado, who was the minister of the Secretariat, and Teresita Maniglia.[4] The first thing we decided was to move the program back to Sunday because more people stay at home that day.

And on Sundays when I am out of the country, we try to record a program or send at least a message. We have done the *Aló presidente* program from the Dominican Republic, from Guatemala.

The other thing was we revised the program's format and to do that we called in the technicians. That was when we decided to make it into a TV show as well as a radio broadcast.

I had to make a real effort to change my style, and to accommodate the different needs of a TV broadcast. So that meant we had to decrease the number of phone calls we accepted because, of course, the TV producers didn't like the idea of putting a little phone icon on the screen every time someone called in. I had to tell them not to cut out the core part of the program—the phone calls were fundamental to our communication strategy.

They are long programs—five, six, or even seven hours long. The record is seven hours.

And why do they have to be so long?

I like it like that. I know some people do not like it and I have made efforts to reduce its length, but the tendency—at the end of the day it is my tendency [he laughs]—has been to make it longer. Anita Rangel got tired of passing me notes: you have twenty minutes, forty minutes, and so on. The viewer ratings stay very high and we have carried out a few polls to verify its popularity.

Do some start watching in the middle?

Yes, my daughter once said to me: "But, Papa, how long is it? I got up, I took my bath listening to you, I went shopping with a few friends and there you were on the TV. And then we came back in the car and turned on the radio, and there you were; I got home and took another bath, and you were still going. How long do you go for? After five hours don't you get tired?" But I like it; I really do enjoy it. And anyway, I feel like I am really communicating with the people.

A lady sent a letter telling me that she was finally able to get her husband to let her watch the program on Sundays. How did she do it? Ironing. She came up with the idea to leave all the clothes for Sunday and then she makes big piles of it so that her husband doesn't try to get her to go out for a walk and she starts ironing when the program begins.

And of course there is the radio, which has much wider penetration. You will even see the guys on the beach listening to it sometimes.

What is the format for the program now?

We changed the format and now it is much more organized. It starts with a video that covers some important aspect of national life; children, ecology, history, or some current event, usually trying to avoid explicitly political themes and focusing on cultural issues, things that are relevant to all Venezuelans. Then I give a talk about the video and open the program. Before, there was a host who ended up supporting the coup, can you imagine? When that host left, we decided that I would take over for him even though I am not a journalist. I *am* a radio announcer, and I have had my degree for fifteen years now.

There is a part of the show dedicated to the agenda for the week, which we now call the National Agenda. Before the April 2002 coup I read my agenda for the week to come : "Monday morning I am gong to be in such and such a place; Tuesday night. . . ." But for security reasons I had to stop making that information public and now we don't even announce where we are going to be broadcasting the next program from. Now we talk about the previous week's schedule.

There is a section called "Good News," because to face the avalanche of negative news that the media publishes we have to publicize the good things that are happening in the country.

I saw that they are running reruns of that section of the show on Channel 8 at night.[5]

That is a new strategy that Rafael Vargas[6] and the team that is in the Secretariat came up with; I was pleasantly surprised. They told me, "Look, we have made a one-hour summary of the show to retransmit it at night during prime time, because five hours on TV is a lot of time."

I usually prepare the program, sometimes I see the videos, other times I don't have time and then I arrive, sit down, and begin to develop it there. At first, I did not have a production team, but now there is one that is really dependable. As soon as we finish one program the team begins working on the next one.

Well, I also have to tell you that the political situation in the country affects the show; sometimes circumstances force us to change the program; sometimes I make mistakes or make comments that are not planned.

One of the criticisms that I have heard is that you announced that you were firing someone on the air.

That is one of the worst mistakes I have made, and moreover, with a whistle [he laughs].

What do you mean with a whistle?

I was really annoyed because they had not fired a person from PDVSA who should have been trustworthy and who was part of the strike against the government. Finally, on a Sunday morning right before the show, I received a list of the people who were being fired. So I took a whistle, it was too much, I am never going to do that again, Marta, I swear it, but I was really upset by the situation . . .

That was not part of the plan . . .

. . . I said "such and such person—dismissed" and then I blew the whistle. And so on down the list. That fell like a bomb on the middle class and professionals. They were offended, as though I had attacked them directly.

But, aside from mistakes like that one and others that you have made on the show, the majority of people recognize that Aló presidente is a veritable school for popular education of the Venezuelan people, that you have used those few hours a week of direct contact with the people to inform them of the government policies, to raise their level of political consciousness.

What can I tell you, Marta? It has been a wonderful experience!

Moving on to another topic, after the April coup, you proposed to open a national dialogue with all the social sectors and political forces and all you asked in return was that they respect the rule of law and therefore the rules set out in the new constitution. But I get the impression that enemies of the process have interpreted this spirit of conciliation as a sign of weakness and that they continue working to overthrow your government and do not have a constructive dialogue. This reminds me of when Lenin and the Bolsheviks took a series of measures to respect the functioning of private property and private companies and their advertising, on the assumption that the Russian bourgeoisie would accept a peaceful coexistence with the revolution. Faced with the benevolent revolutionary strategy, they developed an all-or-nothing strategy of civil war, and they tried to destroy the new command, counting on support from the bourgeoisie in other countries. Do you think this could happen in Venezuela? It would seem that the strategy is to overthrow Chávez and not to construct the country. What balance is there with the dialogue? The view from the outside is that the dialogue has not made any progress.

I do think the dialogue has made progress and has had some results. Of course, as you said, there are some sectors that refuse to participate in dialogue.

Among them is Miquilena.

And a lot of other political factions: the AC, COPEI, and others. But you know, their approach really doesn't make sense. It would be understandable if someone refused to participate in dialogue because their rights had been trampled on, but nothing like that has happened. We have made it more than clear, with both words and deeds, that we are committed to dialogue, so this indicates that they don't have a solid reason for opposing dialogue and that we are talking about an obsession with defending privilege; with getting me out to reactivate the Punto Fijo pact, or some new power-sharing agreement that favors the elites.

No one can deny that we have had attitudes that might be called conciliatory—to put it that way—changes in the directorship of PDVSA, changes of government ministers, new policies, dialogue sessions; the Anzoátegui consensus;[7] the decision to transfer resources to state governments; respect for human rights in the case of the conspirators in the coup.

On the other hand, a lot of groups from national civil society have gotten involved in the dialogue process. And the process has extended to the regional level as well, so we now have regional governors and leaders of local opposition in dialogue even when the national leaders have refused. Not long ago, I was talking on the phone and the governor of Apure came in. Apure is a state that has had a lot of problems with flooding. Well, we had ministers, planes, the military, all working on it because it is something that impacts the whole country; I don't care that the governor there is from the AD and that his party is refusing to dialogue. And the governor said to me: "Look, Mr. President, here I am in a meeting with mayors, there is media here and I am telling them that I am deeply grateful for the national government's support and that I am willing to work for you to help solve all these problems, to find a way out of the country's problems." This governor was from the AD party. And there is another one, the one from Monagas. Add to them mayors, regional directors of COPEI, the church, bishops, regional business association presidents even when they belong to Fedecámaras.[8] They have stepped it up and begun dialogue even when Fedecámaras refuses to participate. In Fedeindustria,[9] in Conindustria[10] there are businessmen who face reality and who don't want to be manipulated into playing an opposition political role but rather who want to run their businesses. We have even had bankers come and say: "Mr. President, we want to work with you to solve the problems with interest rates, credit, the country's economic recovery; we don't want them to manipulate us again." They realized that they were used during the buildup to the coup. I don't think they are totally innocent themselves, but I do believe that there was a lot of pressure and manipulation, that led some people—because of fear, media pressure—to participate in some capacity in the coup.

The media attacked the dialogue from day one. It hasn't mattered at all to the media that we are including people like Janet Kelly—a U.S. citizen and university professor from the IESA [Institute for Advanced Administrative Studies] who has lived here for years, a woman who is critical of the government but has not been a visceral critic as some, like José Luis Betancourt of the cattle farmers, have been.

Marta, I do believe that the dialogue has produced some positive results.

Do you realize what happened on July 11 in that march that they organized? That was evidence of a division in the leadership of the opposition. On the night of July 10, there was a meeting between government representatives and that group, and since then we have noticed the division. Some of them recognized that the government was right, that their march could not go all the way to Miraflores tearing up the city, breaking through police and military barricades, creating chaos all over again. And in the end they were OK with only getting to within a few blocks of Miraflores and then dispersing. Another example of their divisions was when a group of the rabid opposition decided to go over to La Carlota, the Caracas air base, for an action later that day. Some leaders of the very same opposition came out against that action. I believe that is related to our efforts at dialogue, which have been making progress.

CHAPTER SEVEN

A Political Party at Its Height

You were telling me that if a great social force is unleashed but not channeled it can end up being destructive and sometimes even self-destructive, anarchistic, as has happened in many countries. On the other hand, you have repeatedly stated that you agree with what I put forward in my book The Left in the Twenty-first Century: Making Possible the Impossible, *about how politics is the art of building the force to make possible in the future what seems impossible in the moment. How do you envision the construction of that force?*

Back in '93 we were saying that the people were the fuel for the machinery of history. We also said that to have a people, from the sociological, social-political perspective, it isn't enough to have twenty or forty million people in a certain area. To have a people there must be a common sense of identity. A historian once talked about drinking from the collective fountain, or having a project in common, a common dream; to have a common thread that unites the great majority of the citizens in that area.

For a long time the Venezuelan people did not have a consciousness, they were divided, they did not have a common project; they were a people without hope, without direction. More than being a people, we were a collection of human beings, but then, as a result of the historical process that our country has undergone over the last few decades, a people has been formed. We are talking about awakening a giant.

Now, that awakening was not enough. It was crucial that the people organize themselves; it was crucial that the unprecedented popular force be unified and strengthened so instead of moving forward along thousands of individual paths, it found a common direction. We needed to give the people direction so that they could increase their level of organization, ideology, and capacity for combat. At that time we had national leadership that had come together in prison, but we did not want it to become an extreme hierarchy where a few of us decided everything, without paying attention to anyone else. We sought out organizing models to convert the popular movement into a bottom-up avalanche.

When we got out of prison we began to develop a few organizational theories to help the massive support movement, still informal, take shape. We spent hours debating, comparing organizational models. We organized workshops, forums.

A team dedicated itself to considering a range of organizational models and then presented the rest of us with various alternatives. We were able to make good progress even though MBR 200 was initially being persecuted, almost [made] illegal, and declared to be subversive; its leaders were being watched and many of them detained. That was when we decided to create the Bolivarian committees as the base structure of the movement. They were small, almost clandestine groups. We traveled the whole country with that organizational proposal and put it to the people, the communities, the neighborhoods. We reinitiated the idea of the committees later, during the constitutional assembly process, but with a new name: Bolívarian Circles.

That effort to organize was not a political party and there was a lot of opposition to the idea of converting the movement into a party.

But, how was that movement structured?

We had regional coordinators and a national coordinator. The situation did not allow for an open procedure to democratically elect the leadership. It was a *sui generis* movement in a special situation from 1994–96.

We were not trying to put totally original ideas into practice, they came from a range of experiences, they reflected lessons learned from previous mistakes. We knew that we had to be paying attention to the masses, to avoid losing our connection with them. We wanted to build a process that was truly driven from below.

Where did the idea for the MVR party come from?

The idea to convert the MBR 200 into the MVR to enter the 1998 elections came out of an intense debate because the MBR 200 was in a process of radicalization and in 1996 when we put forward the idea of entering electoral politics—as I was telling you earlier—there was a sharp reaction from within the movement as it was not a party and did not have a party structure or electoral ambitions.

It was during an MBR 200 National Assembly held in Valencia on April 19, 1997, that we decided to take the electoral route. The idea was to maintain the MBR 200 profile and project [it], but [also] to transform the movement into the central motor of an electoral campaign, which was called the MVR. We never thought that MBR 200 would disappear, but rather that it would become the driving force behind the political party.

When exactly was the MVR established?

The MVR is a party that was established at a very carefully determined political moment: the 1999 elections for the constitutional assembly. It went on to participate in the rest of the electoral processes in 2000. It was formed at the height of an electoral process and it was not held back by being a clandestine struggle. Since it was born in the midst of an avalanche of support [for Chávez] a lot of ambitious, duplicitous, hangers-on came around. We knew that might happen; it was part of the risk we knew we were taking.

But this was a party that was founded for the elections; the first thing the people did was prepare for the elections, the tactics, and perhaps we forgot the strategy. On the other hand, a good number of our core leadership took on responsibilities: they became governors, mayors, representatives, ambassadors. They found themselves committed to a system complete with an antiquated bureaucratic apparatus that was extremely limiting.

This also happened to me. From '94 until '97 I was a political leader who dedicated my time to organizing the movement, to studying, to developing strategy, ideology, doctrine, tactics, but when I was elected president, where was the time for all that supposed to come from? As president of the party I had to learn to delegate almost all the political party responsibilities.

As a result of this situation, we felt like the MVR was becoming bureaucratized and losing its connection with the masses. It got heavy, ungainly, Marta. Disconcerting elements began to appear, for example, people in the regions began to complain that their leaders were not attending to their needs, that there were lots of internal divisions and rivalries.

I felt like the party did not have what it took for the new strategic situation we were facing: a phase where we had to deepen the process. I am talking about 2001, when we began the phase of the empowerment laws. I was aware that we needed to use those laws to transform the country and that there would naturally be a reaction, which is exactly what happened. Being president of the party at that time was like being behind the wheel of a car going uphill, putting the pedal to the metal, and yet not going anywhere. Of course there were also internal contradictions developing.

The streets and the neighborhoods and the regions had become terribly cold politically. People complained that the party had lost contact with the people. I felt it because, as you know, I avoided locking myself up in Miraflores. And that process chilled me to the core.

So the party began a theoretical debate: was it going to be a party for its members or for the masses?

The mayors and governors were not fulfilling their roles because all the people's complaints and problems were coming to me: "I am sick," "I don't have anywhere to sleep . . . " An extraordinary amount of work fell into my hands. I had to develop a series of ad hoc teams to deal with problems that local governments should have been dealing with. Where were the party members that should have been helping all those people?

In spite of all this, we can't forget that the MVR fulfilled a very important role in the 1999 constitutional assembly struggle and again in 2000 in the process to relegitimize the government under the new constitution. It conducted seven electoral campaigns and we won them all.

This worrisome situation facing the MVR motivated us to announce the relaunching of the MBR 200 on April 25, 2001. It was an idea that some had been advocating for quite a while.

They say that you made that idea public without consulting with anyone. Is that true?

I made the announcement as the result of a reflection process that did not involve consulting with or debate within the party—that is true. Now, I remember when I made the announcement I got a standing ovation, everyone was clapping over there in the assembly, including the people from our party. The main point in my talk was about the need to regenerate the movement of the masses. This announcement took everyone by surprise and, as always, the opposition media began to manipulate the situation: "That Chávez declared the MVR dead and he is bringing back the violent military-based MBR 200." Of course, my announcement worried some people. The truth is it was never my idea to make the MVR disappear. I think an important group of the leaders understood it and followed its direction. At that moment I put forward a general idea, but then I said: "We have to design the methodology, the tactics to reactivate the popular movement, the Bolívarian Circles."

The work that started after that, in spite of all the imperfections and contradictions it has had, allowed us to respond to the general strike that the opposition began on December 10. That day there was an extremely important popular response to the call for the strike.

My talk ended up providing quite a jolt, and it even forced the party to take on its responsibilities in terms of popular work that it had abandoned. In addition, it revitalized the party's support bases and thus began an interwoven support process.

A few months after the relaunching of the MBR 200, on December 17, 2001, I made it clear in another talk that we were not going to let the MVR disappear, but rather that we had to turn it around and strengthen it so that it could serve as one of the primary motors to drive and orient the process.

We made it clear that the MBR 200 was not a party nor was it the patrimony of any party; it was the people organizing to defend and drive forward the revolution. We used the example of drops of water. I said that each one of us was like a drop of water and when unified with other drops of water we could form a stream, and lots of streams together could form a great river. A Bolívarian Circle could be made of seven people, ten people, fifteen people; there should be a Circle on every corner, in every neighborhood, in every town, in the petroleum fields, in the factories, in the schools, in the technical schools, in the Bolívarian schools, in the *bodegas*, in indigenous communities. There should be Bolívarian circles all over and they should build social networks out of these circles, and a network of these networks forms streams that together form the transformational river of our movement. There are already many but they need to be much stronger, like, for example, the Bolívarian workers' groups. There are Bolívarian women's groups, youth groups, farmers' groups, and all of them united, form the MBR 200. It is this movement that is going to guarantee, in spite of all the risks and dangers, that the revolutionary process is deepened and consolidated.

The basic nuclei of the MBR 200 are the Bolívarian Circles and forces. These organizations, as I was saying, go beyond, transcend political parties.

The Bolívarian forces were born out of the same process and have grouped themselves on the basis of social sectors. There are MVR militants there, people from the PCV, the PPT, but the majority of them are people who do not belong to any party. That is another part of our reality, our people had been disconnected from the country's political parties for so long that a lot of them had a hard time accepting the MVR because they see it as just another party.

This process created lots of dynamics—there are popular networks all over, there are cultural organizations, environmental groups, unions—it is amazing how the unions have been organized over the last few years! Well, the Bolívarian Circles are simply a manifestation of constituent power in action.

What concrete work do the Bolívarian Circles do?

They have a range of responsibilities: for example, they work in their communities, taking care of the elderly; working on ecology projects, planting trees; they work in their neighborhoods protecting citizens and the public order, fighting crime. . . .

And I want to make clear that the government does not finance the Bolívarian Circles. I have suggested that they take collections, [find] ways to finance themselves, perhaps through production and consumption cooperatives. They should invent some way to fund them because the people's greatest power is their own intelligence, force, and energy.

Why has the Right condemned them so harshly?

Because they have grown really strong and the thing the Right fears most is an organized people. That is why they have a systematic campaign against the circles; they practice a kind of terrorism, portraying them as violent paramilitary groups. But this smear campaign has failed to weaken the circles; if anything, it has strengthened them.

Can you clear something up for me? If the MBR 200 becomes the MVR and that party is, as you have said, a party that attracts a lot of opportunists and so on, if half of the members of the party are not deeply committed, if they are not members who are willing to put themselves at risk in defense of the process—as the media in Venezuela indicates to be the case—how can that party be the right tool to direct the revolutionary process?

I would not put it so harshly. I would tell you that if we compare the leading members of the MBR 200 up until '97 with those from the MVR today, I would say that they are basically the same. I mean, what was the local, regional, and national leadership is still involved in the leadership today. At the national level: William Lara, Iris Varela, Cilia Flores, Pedro Carreño, and many more are still key leaders and are among the hardest, firmest legislators we have. And the governors: Reyes Reyes, Florencio Porras, Blanco La Cruz, who separated from us after getting out of prison, but who was with us in the beginning, and Hilmer Viloria; and there is my father, who got involved with the movement when I was imprisoned. Adan, my brother, Freddy Bernal, and lots of other members who work with him; the mayor of Barquisimeto. All of them were founders of the movement and lots more are working with the government today.

The point is, the nucleus of the MBR 200 is within the MVR and it has been one of the driving forces in the party. Of course you have people like Miquilena who rose to power but they were eventually forced out by loyal party members.

Of course what you say is also true, there are people who have no scruples, no ideology, without a revolutionary commitment who take advantage, but the process naturally excludes them, cuts them off. After the coup—and this is a positive occurrence—an internally reflexive process, a corrective process began to develop; there is a social impulse that rises from the people, from beyond party politics.

You told me that you were a chief without a staff, I think the way in which you relaunched the MBR 200 is evidence of that, but I understand that you have wanted to build that staff, is that right? What effort have you made in this area over the last three years? Have you been able to work in teams? Who makes up those teams?

I confess, Marta, I am a tough guy. If you work directly with me, we might fight, you would realize how hard I am to work with. That is one of the things about me, and I have made efforts to improve in this area.

Why is it hard to work with you?

I am extremely demanding. I complain, and hold people accountable, and that high level of expectation can push people away, or push me away from others. I really must avoid this because I ought to create conditions that allow people to improve as a team, to correct mistakes. I like teamwork, I don't like being alone—I don't think many people like it—and anyone who has worked with me has experienced a demanding *jefe*, sometimes an implacable one. I think that makes it harder to work with me. I have had teams, of course, and I still have teams. Sometimes, when something doesn't work out, I say I don't have a team, but of course I do. I told you I didn't have a staff, but I do and not just one, many: the cabinet, the council of ministers, the policy team from the party, the economic team, and the revolutionary political command. They haven't all worked out as well as they should have for a lot of reasons, some of which are structural.

Structural? In what sense?

For example, sometimes the ministers are almost totally absorbed in their space, in their structure, by their plans and internal dynamics, by the failures of the state structure and so that makes it hard to have an integrated team. The ministers have a tendency to isolate themselves in their own area. That is one of the problems, aside from my own shortcomings, that we have had.

Your shortcomings?

I often create a tough working dynamic and an irregular schedule. Once, someone said to me: "you really must organize your schedule more scientifically." My schedule is so irregular, so changeable that it makes it hard for anyone who works with me to maintain their own schedules in any kind of an orderly fashion. Sometimes something is planned for one day and I flip it all around and upside down. I don't do it senselessly, a lot of times they are necessary, justifiable changes. But a lot of times the people who work with me don't understand the changes and I don't know how to explain it to them and this creates tension in our team.

But more than that, Marta, I think the dynamic is overwhelming and that creates its own problems. Some people criticize me because of the major changes I make, but sometimes you have to advance through trial and error. PDVSA, for example, has had five presidents, not including the current one, but that is because we did not find someone who could successfully manage the technical and political responsibility of managing a government entity of such national importance. A few months ago I named Ali Rodriguez to the position and I am confident that he is the man for the job.

I have changed several ministers and vice ministers. Sometimes it is hard to find a person with both the qualities that Maneiro talked about: political efficiency and revolutionary quality, or what Matus refers to as the techno-political. Sometimes you have a great politician, but then when it comes to the technical side, or to management in a certain area, they begin to show their weaknesses. I have had and continue to have wonderful ministers. But I have had others who I believed were going to do a good job and they did not whether because of individualism, because they wanted to work only with the team they were used to working with, or because they fought for the same approach for many years and felt that now was the time to put it into action, even if their approach did not coincide with the general strategy of the government. So, in those cases, there were problems with other ministries or directors and sometimes with me as well. I feel terrible sometimes when I have to fire people because they don't understand the process that we are undergoing; they have a different perspective. In short, there are a series of causes that explain this rotation in the government, which I know to be problematic.

There are those who say you lead like an officer from the military.

That is true. Perhaps that reflects my deep desire to move something important forward, but I don't think I am like that with major government issues. I like to delegate responsibility. It is hard to find a ministry who says I am all over them, sometimes they complain because I leave them alone too much, or don't attend to certain things. My style is quite different from the classic military method that is limited to giving orders and going around people. I delegate a lot; if you interview people who work with me they can confirm what I am saying. I like doing it in almost any field so that people develop initiative and learn responsibility. Sometimes I have delegated too much responsibility to people like Miquilena or to certain groups that have made decisions without consulting with me, and when I find out, sometimes it is too late to put it in reverse and fix something done poorly. The military is the area in which I delegate the least.

You have mentioned the Revolutionary Political Command[1] as part of your staff and you have explained—when you swore them in, in January 2002,[2]—that your idea was this command would work with those responsible for moving the process forward in various areas of the government: governors, mayors, ministers, representatives, and so forth, when previously everyone did their own thing. You maintained that this central command was particularly important in the complicated political phase to deepen the revolutionary process against the efforts of the Right. You indicated the need to plan battles to lead the people to victory. You felt that in order to be successful, this command would need to be clear on the context, where the process was headed, what the goals and objectives of the revolution are. You recalled that the revolutionary project has five strategic axes: the political that builds the Bolivarian democracy; the economic that builds a humane, sustainable, diversified, productive economic system; the social that seeks to get rid of the social debt and establish social justice—the ultimate goal of the revolution; the territorial that seeks to decentralize power and balance development throughout the country; and finally,

the international that strengthens our sovereignty within the frame-
work of a multipolar world. You said that the National Assembly
accepted these five grand axes of the national project of the revolution
and so the main thing now was to put them into practice. To accom-
plish this with political efficiency, you insisted that it was necessary
to get past individual self-interest, party interests, rivalries, and so
on. You said that it was necessary to take the helm of the revolution-
ary ship and bring all the parties together. In this political project,
where does your anti-party attitude fit?

I have criticized certain political parties for their attitudes, but that
doesn't mean I condemn the political parties. On the contrary, I
want there to be a party that keeps up with the process.

How do you envision that party?

It should be a party that is appropriate for the revolutionary
process that we are fighting for and for the world reality in which
that fight is taking place.

Just as a military organization needs to be flexible enough to
adapt to a changing reality—you can't have an armored unit that is
rigid, that is incapable of changing, of preparing for different combat situations whether in the jungle or in the desert; in the winter or
summer—a political party should be able to adapt to the demands
of reality. Today, for example, the party, whether we are talking
about the MVR, the PPT, the MAS,[3] the PCV, any of those, if there
is an electoral challenge the party should be capable of rising to that
challenge and winning the elections. Then, after the election, the
party should work on other projects.

Let's suppose that as a result of the electoral campaign, the party
holds some positions: a mayor's office, a governorship, a local council. The party should transform those spaces into a base of operations, into an instrument to begin applying their ideology, their theory. They should begin to transform the concept and praxis of the
government. They should put in place a new form of government:
toward the people, for the people, and with the people. They should

promote popular participation. Depending on the specifics, the timing, the level of government and support for the revolution will be more or less superficial, more or less deep. From our point of view, at the presidential level, we are applying a critical analysis based on our ideological viewpoint. Governors and mayors should do the same.

Now, there are other political situations that are different in that you are not working from a position of power. In those cases the party should adapt to particulars of the situation. In a municipality where they do not govern, the party should get deeply involved in popular organizing, it should bring even more support to popular movements, popular consciousness, including their ideology and strategic vision. This does not mean that in areas they do control they should stop doing all these things, but it is less of a necessity.

Of course a political party should have a strategic plan that it follows. Organizing the popular movement should be an everyday job, especially in a revolutionary party. And it should use any mechanisms available to it whether or not it controls the government. I remember that while we were in prison, we read some of Gramsci's work. Gramsci said that a party that aspires to lead society should be leaders, before coming to power, in the classical sense of power.

We do not have a party or parties like that, but, Marta, you also can't say that we don't have any of that. There are political leaders at the local and national level—not just from the MVR—that are doing a very good job.

We have begun a transition from a few parties working in the electoral sphere to a few parties working for a revolution, for a popular organization with a clear ideology, supporting the masses through the work of well-trained party members. We must develop this and work at this much more, but we aren't starting from scratch, we have advanced in this area.

Perhaps the solution to constructing the political instrument we need could be the creation of an environment that goes beyond party politics and to propose a unified movement, a popular Bolívarian bloc. That is part of what we are looking for.

You insist that party members in the government should promote
popular participation as one of their primary responsibilities, but
people complain that a lot of members do nothing of the kind.

It has to work with those that are here. The political and social
dynamic that is necessary to solve these problems will come. People's participation could solve a lot of these problems: if that guy
doesn't work, if the other one didn't show up. . . . When the majority of the community is participating, those leaders will be obligated to change, or they will be rejected. I believe that.

The constitution talks about community assemblies, whose decisions have weight as defined within the Law of Participation. For
example, in Trujillo, a municipality's assembly decided to fire the
mayor and they went right to his office with all the signatures.
Although what they did was not in accordance with the law, I am
telling you about it because it reflects the results of the constitutional process, the people's newfound spirit of participation. People no
longer go about their day bitter or downtrodden. Now the spirit of
participation has gained momentum and not always exactly as the
constitution describes, but often spontaneously. Here in Caracas, for
example, there are community water organizations, which existed
prior to the new constitution but that have been reactivated.

Now, I don't think that all the mayors are indifferent to participation. I have seen some support participation, for example, here
in Caracas, Freddy Bernal. He has conceptualized and put in place
some important policies that promote neighborhood-level participation. He has worked with youth brigades; he is supporting
urban planning committees. And, over there in Sucre, in Barquisimeto, and countless other parts of the country, the same
kinds of things are happening.

Here in Caracas there are two projects underway that are like
pilot participation projects—they are the ones I have seen, but there
are lots of others—Las Malvinas and El Winche. I mentioned the Las
Malvinas project to you, where we were with Mayor Freddy Bernal.
We had a meeting with the community leaders of that troubled area,

discussing proposals, projects, complaints, accomplishments. Then we went to see one of the projects that the community is doing with funding that they control through cooperatives, neighborhood associations, and with the support of Plan Bolívar. They are rehabilitating their neighborhood, building common spaces, practicing sports. They have a community radio station and have asked for permission to have another one.

The other example was in El Winche, at the other end of the city in the municipality of Sucre. There the mayor was José Vicente Rangel. That is one of the most depressed zones economically, in Petare. Recently we did an *Aló presidente* there. The president of the Community Development Council was there and she participated in the program. I asked her if she was in charge and she gave me an extraordinary response. "I am not in charge. No one is in charge here, Mr. President. We have a horizontal organization." "Ah, very well, I tell her, look, you have surprised me, explain a bit more." "OK, there are no managers here, there is a coordinator, but this is a development council that has been around for a year. The mayors never came by or paid attention to us and then one time some people with T-shirts from the mayor's office in Sucre came by and distributed pamphlets and a card inviting us to a meeting. We got together and they told us we were brought together to form the development council, following what the mayor instructed, and that he would be arriving shortly.

In the meeting to form that council there were some seven hundred people, a huge number for that neighborhood, and it was those people who appointed the board of directors. They are organizing around new housing units that are being built; they participate in the design and everything. They are also the ones who work to solve major problems like dealing with the water supply in the neighborhood. They don't have running water there, so a truck goes up every twenty days to fill the tanks that each family uses. They realized that they could tap into the water stored at a nearby dam. Their idea was taken up by the mayor with support from Plan Bolívar, Plan Caracas, and the minister of the environment. They did a study to see if the plan was feasible, and it was. They completed the project within a year, so the neighborhood now has water.

They are also going to have a school and an athletic field. They are working on community-based ways to process yuca, and so on. I mean, in that neighborhood you see the constitutional approach to participatory democracy put into practice, participation made into a reality.

There are other similar projects in the neighborhood called January 23 in Catia. They are projects that are just putting down roots and getting started.

We have to be constantly working more and more closely with popular organizations do a better job hearing their criticism, their ideas, their suggestions, because who better than the popular organizations to control the action of the government at every level? I could be tricked—I have only two eyes, but when every Venezuelan becomes conscious, we all become vigilantes for the small municipal projects as well as major development work. The people can see the failures, where the local or national governments have been infiltrated, etc. We have to be very vigilant because there is an immense capacity for turncoats. This is one of the biggest problems facing a peaceful revolution like ours.

I have requested information from popular organizations, especially recommendations to help me make progressive, well thought out, timely, and efficient decisions.

We must do more than the constitutional minimum in terms of concrete projects, and there is nothing better than community participation to support work in areas like education, health care, employment, and so on.

We are talking about leadership that promotes popular participation, but people are quick to accuse you of being a populist, a strongman. Although you try to organize the people, empower them, support the rise of local leadership, one of the most important failures of the process has been its inability to form a single strategic command of the revolution. On the other hand, I know that you can't

close your eyes to the fact that you are a myth, a legend for the peo-
ple. I also know that you have made it clear you want to transform
the movement into a myth, not the other way around. This is not
about substituting a dictator or a messiah for the movement, but
rather about transforming "the masses that were immobile, amor-
phous into a massive movement." Nonetheless, don't you think that
you have a demeanor that encourages that myth? For example, the
program Aló presidente, *which we have already talked about,*
where anyone who contacts Chávez can resolve their problems.

You are, however, a people person. When I went with you to do
the program Aló presidente *and to dedicate a school and a medical*
center in Puerto Cruz, I saw how you treated the people, how their
problems genuinely interest you. You spent several hours doing this
stuff, and when I saw you, I thought you would move on to promot-
ing organizing discussions with the community, to encourage the
people to talk through their problems, and search for solutions. I
remember that in one of the local governments I studied you received
a group of people to hear their demands, but only if they did it in an
organized manner, in which case the solution could come out of
community action.

Let me defend myself; let's use an example from today in Puerto
Cruz. My attitude there was not in contradiction with the strategy
of building an organized force, of encouraging participation. Now, I
do think we need to analyze, criticize, and improve upon the
methodology, the approach to this work. I will repeat, this does not
go against the idea of participation, it is a way to put participation
theory into practice. Let me review a few examples from today. We
got off the helicopter, you probably noticed that some cars were
waiting to take us to the site, and I decided to walk instead. You
saw the people awaiting my arrival, hoping I would greet them and
I could not resist the urge to talk to them. So a visit scheduled for
two hours like today's ended up being a full day.

But yes, we do need a better approach. I remember that when Fidel
came and saw how people came up to me and passed me notes, asking

*for things, he told them: "Chávez can't be the mayor of all of
Venezuela, you guys are gonna kill him."*

Let me tell you, Marta, journalists from all over the world and
some have traveled with me, as you are doing now. The thing is at
this particular moment, you are seeing me in a phase where I am
working almost like a social guerrilla. I show up sometimes without any advance warning, even this morning, they didn't know if I
would come or not.[4]

First of all, it was way too much for us; we were going crazy
with so many little requests. Now we have entered a new phase, we
have been developing a new methodology. We have a guy who carries a computer and processes all the requests we get in the office
in the palace where there are some forty people working: lawyers,
sociologists, mostly young people who organize the requests
around housing issues, farming issues, employment, health. . . .
Then, some of those problems can be converted into popular
organizing tools, and I insist on that, you saw it this morning with
the bankrupt woman who cleans the health clinic and is losing her
house, she came to me with her personal problems and so I proposed that tomorrow or the next day there be a housing commission to study the problem that is so common amongst the people,
because I know there are other people with similar problems. So
that is how we came up with projects like Plan Wasp, which I told
you about earlier.

There is a marine captain who is in charge of one of the Plan Bolívar projects on the coast, and I talked to him for a little while. They
get involved in their local community, ideally to hear the community's
needs so that they can collaborate in developing community projects.
The nice little health clinic that we saw is an example of that collaboration. Since that area is really hot, it is elevated, and has a central
patio to help circulate the air; the school is the same. We don't use the
same design for public buildings all over the country anymore; now
we build them to meet the local needs and circumstances. I can't guarantee you that the construction of that community project has includ-

ed x percent of community participation, but several things I saw and heard suggest that it was a participatory project.

It has been tough for me because I have to motivate people to express their ideas, so that the projects develop along the lines of their needs, so that we are not the ones designing the projects in a central office and then going out there and doing it on our own. No, first we go there to talk to the people.

You saw that they are planting crops in the hills. It is not that the land there is particularly good for agriculture, but they say it is good and that means it is good for them, so we are not going to undo their work. We cannot decree from above that they not plant in a certain area. An agricultural technician should come and ask them what they have produced and they should carry out a scientific study on the ground there to find out how good the soil is and if it is better for rice, squash, or watermelon. Then, on that basis, they can be given a micro-credit. Sometimes they aren't given money because people have so many needs that they spend it on other things, so instead they are given the tools for their work—rakes, hoes, axes, machetes—and they get offered a course that helps orient them toward cooperative work. The constitution talks about how Venezuela's socioeconomic regime ought to be strongly based around cooperative and associative work and that this will help break free of individualism and neoliberalism, which gives the program a strong socialist content. To cooperativize is to socialize the economy, give it social content. I am confident that in Puerto Cruz they are going to develop agricultural cooperatives.

Today, a man asked me for a four-by-four [truck] because he could not get his agricultural products out of his mountain town and so it all went to waste. What did I say to the people in charge there? Look, we cannot give this man a four-by-four but we can give it to an agricultural cooperative. We have to encourage them to organize with others into a cooperative and when they register we will give them that four-by-four, but not to him as an individual. And maybe they can even get a microcredit to help commercialize their production.

You have seen only a part of this new method, the first part, where we record people's problems. And there are individual personal

problems, like someone who has stomach cancer and needs an operation, or a kid who has leg problems and can't walk, these are really
painful cases. But when it comes to how we respond, we always try to
include social content as a strategic orientation. Today, for example,
that school we inaugurated, ought to be more than just a place for
kids to study math and reading, it should be a community action center. The computers should not only be used by students, but rather
they should also serve the people of that town. It is a revolution for
those people in that small town to have access to a computer. They
are already writing things, learning. The health clinic should also
become a community action center.

Now, in your question, you referred to the myth of Chávez, and
that does exist, though I never did anything to promote it. Arias Car-
denas was one of those who accused me of encouraging the myth and
I told him that it was not my fault, that it came about as a result of my
television appearance in '92 when I said "for now."

When I got out of prison, one of the things I thought to myself
was that if that myth existed, I was going to destroy it. And as president I have been demystifying everything. It has not been easy.
During my first few days and months as president, the people were
surging forward with emotion and passion. Several times when I
went to sit down somewhere people came running from all over,
fighting past the soldiers to meet me.

A lot of them just wanted to touch me, give me a note, or tell me
something. You can imagine that such a flood of people makes it
pretty tough to have meetings or assemblies in an orderly fashion.
Nonetheless, I agree with you: that element is missing, at least in
my more restricted activities, my work meetings.

I really do not believe that this work is producing a people com-
prised of beggars. I don't see it that way because our attitude is not
like some governments that show up with a bag full of money and start
giving it out—that was populism. I am totally against that. We are dealing with collecting and processing people's necessities. And processing that information allows us to have a database of all the people we
have helped with housing, land, micro-credits, to be able to evaluate

our work a few years from now, and the level of social organization that results from our approach.

Nora Castañeda, for example, is an excellent revolutionary who directs the women's bank. I remember when I appointed her, I said to her, "Nora, I am going to assign you presidential funds so you can get started." She replied, "No, we don't need money just yet, we are going to start with courses and workshops." That bank does not give credit to any woman who has not had course work, especially on social and community-based work.

I am putting pressure so that we can also move the revolution into housing, that is to say, so that we give greater social value to housing issues. We are going to the poorest parts, and to middle-class sectors as well where there is the most need to organize OCVs (community housing organizations). We have to try to make a lot of progress in community projects. Now I am going to create the ministry of housing and separate it from the ministry of infrastructure, which is a massive ministry in charge of water, air, and land transportation, housing, neighborhoods, and so on.

In Caracas there is a neighborhood called the Malvinas—a neighborhood high up on a hill in the Caracas Valley—that I have heard wonders about. There is a project there that General García Carneiro[5] is working on with Nelson Merentes, the ex-minister of science and technology, who is always very much involved in the social component. The community there has organized themselves to fix up their streets and their houses, and I have been encouraging them to find small plots of land around their houses so that they can at least produce what they need to consume, so that they can raise chickens, have a small shed, plant tomatoes. . . .

The point is I believe that we are moving in the right direction, but a lot of people don't understand the depth of the process that is generated through my contact with the people. But as you have seen, it goes way beyond just receiving notes.

CHAPTER EIGHT

The April 11 Coup

Since we are doing this interview in the same place that you were
detained during the April 11 coup, could you tell me your strongest
memories of those bitter hours?

We initially thought we would have several alternatives, including
moving to Maracay, but the tanks I had sent for earlier, needed to
make that move...[under pressure from the generals supporting the
coup] ... had been sent to Fort Tiuna instead. That made our move
to Maracay impossible. After consulting with some of my people, I
finally decided to accept their demand to hand myself in.

I gave Giordani and Navarro hugs and I said good-bye to my
dispatch, saying, "The strategic window has closed." They did not
respond. I thought I was going to die. That ominous feeling
crossed my mind for a few moments. I said good-bye to everyone
who was with me there in the palace.

I went to Fort Tiuna with Generals Rosendo [Manuel Antonio
Rosendo], Hurtado [Ismael Hurtado], and a few others that I
chose. I did not go as a prisoner. It was only when I entered the
building under the command of the general of the army that I
became a prisoner of the coup-mongering generals.

When I was in Fort Tiuna, and I saw on television that an official there had lent me that they announced my resignation, and I
figured out their plot, their lie. Then I thought, they are going to

kill me; it's the only way to prevent me from telling the truth. In that moment, an official lent me a telephone and I called my wife and said to her, "get going, they are about to kill me." I tried calling my daughters and I got one of them, my daughter María, and I told her, "María, get going and spread the word because they are going to kill me."

I also thought they were going to kill you. I still don't understand why they didn't.

They gave the order to kill me, but what happened was the mutinous generals did not have a true leader and some of them, especially the younger officers who were in charge of me, blocked that order.

There was even a waiter, one of those guys who serve coffee, who overheard two officers talking. Apparently he heard Admiral Molina who it seems was pressuring Carmona to order my physical elimination. This young waiter tells me he overheard perfectly when Carmona said, "OK, it's all right, rub him out." And really, that night they took me up to Turiamo in a helicopter—an inhospitable site, given the circumstances, the tensions in that environment—I said to myself, "The moment has come," and I began to recite my prayers with my crucifix. I was ready to die standing, with my dignity. I told myself, "Your hour has come, but you will die for being loyal to your people."

All the lower-ranking people who were around me at each of the various places they had me detained—soldiers and officers alike—went way out of their way to help me out, to clean the room, the modest bathroom. There was a really small bed and they found a better one, and brought a chair. They would offer me sodas, or coffee. They really went out of their way.

When they let me out to take a quick jog, they brought me a T-shirt and they got me some sandals to wear outside, they were ready to help me with whatever little thing I might need.

There were also the two female military prosecutors. These women came into my room by themselves at first, but right after they arrived, they were ordered out and a few minutes later they came back with a colonel from the coup who was a lawyer, and they sat down. So I figured out they had ordered the women out because that officer wanted to be there.

We talked for a few minutes and they asked me how I felt. I told them the first thing I wanted them to know was that I had not renounced or even thought about stepping down. I called out the lie that was being propagated through the media.

The women wrote by hand on a small page a few notes about my health, and I signed it. I saw that they had not written down what I said about not having resigned, but I knew they were under a lot of pressure, and I didn't want to make it worse for them, so I just said, "Well, thanks."

Their look showed me sympathy and they left. You know what they did? After they signed and the colonel looked it over, one of them wrote at the bottom in small letters, "He declared that he has not resigned the presidency." Then they sent a copy of it by fax to the attorney general and that is why Isaías Rodríguez, the DA, in that interview that came out in the afternoon said, "We have received information from the military attorney that the president has not resigned."

Then there is the help I received from the soldier who gave me a rock to pray with. This man was a patriot, in his own way. And the lieutenant who came to Turiamo and told me: "Don't worry, you are our President, don't worry because later tonight we are going to capture the higher officials and get you out of here." There was another guy who showed up once in a while where they had me detained and took notes I wrote out in the garbage, gave them to his wife who made lots of copies, and distributed them showing people that I had not resigned.

All those were a help, one drop after the other. I will never forget those guys, those days.

Being here on Orchid Island today makes me remember two things: one good and one bad. The good memory is I was here during *Semana Santa* swimming with my daughter Rosa Inés, with

María Isabel,[1] and the boy Raúl. I escaped and we had a really nice time. The bad one is that night when I was held prisoner here.

Once night fell, I started to realize that something was happening in the country, something in support of the revolution. I noticed it in the attitude of the soldiers that were watching me. They had undergone a change; I started to feel it in the environment. An admiral came to the island in a helicopter and entered the room I was in—he took off his shoes, dressed in shorts and a T-shirt, eating fish after having taken a run with the men on the island—he stands up straight and says to me, "Mr. President, I come here on a special mission." That was another sign, because that was the first time since I had been taken prisoner that they had called me "President." Then the coup conspirators sent me a special group of emissaries: a general from military justice, a colonel from the coup conspirators, and the archbishop. I was in the little room and was already processing scenarios in my mind about what this group would want with me. I wanted to play for time more than anything else, to try to figure out what was happening in the country. I had allowed them to take me to the island because I know the island—I knew that, in spite of the fact that it was an island, I would have opportunities to get access to information. I even thought if the situation wasn't changing, they were coming to offer me safe passage out of the country and that maybe I should accept, without resigning, the idea of going to a friendly country and then organizing an international action. I wanted to speak with the archbishop first and I told him they made me come here and we talked a few things over. More than anything, I was asking him how it was possible that the Catholic church had allowed a coup that went against the laws of God. We spoke for a little while. Then we went out to the meeting with the others. They had come to bring me the resignation papers to sign and they told me there was a plane waiting to take me out of the country as soon as I signed it. Two nights earlier they had said that it did not matter if I signed, that it was the same anyway. When I saw this I said to myself, "They are in trouble. Something serious is happening if they are coming here and putting a plane at my command."

I told them I could not sign it, that they knew I had been willing to sign under a series of conditions, and I repeated the conditions that I had put forward at the palace. I knew they couldn't give them to me. I told them that the first one was the physical safety of all the people in the country and the government: "You have violated that condition, you have detained people, beat them up, who knows all that is happening now, but while I was at Fort Tiuna, I saw that they had taken Tarek [Williams] prisoner, and also another representative, they had been dragged out of their houses, arrested."

"Second: that they respect the Constitution, that is, if I resign, it must be before the National Assembly, and the vice president assumes the presidency, until they can call new elections. And you guys cancelled the constitution, dissolved the National Assembly, the Supreme Court, and so forth. So what are we really talking about here?

And you knew about all that?

I knew because in Fort Tiuna, as I told you, an official lent me a TV, so all day while I was there, I watched the news, until 6 P.M. Then, when they took me to another location that night, I didn't learn anything else. I had seen that they had taken several people prisoner: the minister of the interior, the governor of Táchira; I saw the self-swearing-in by Carmona, and his decrees.[2]

The third condition was to be able to speak live to the country. "Do you guys really think I am going to leave like that? Without saying anything to the country?"

And fourth: that all my government aides be allowed to come with me; those folks who were with me for years. They were not going to accept that either because that was my support in the whole process.

And the archbishop said: "OK, Chávez, you have to think about the country," you know, with that rhetoric… "I am thinking about the country." We started to argue, and I was buying time the whole while. I saw the sergeants who were there with their rifles and light missiles, talking to each other and looking at me as well; there was a kind of tension in the air. And outside, the admiral who had brought me here was making calls, going in and out. I could tell something was happening, something bigger than the lie about the resignation.

So I focused on buying time, on talking and debating. That is when I put forward a second scenario; I told them, "Look, I am not going to sign the resignation. You guys have violated the constitution," and I showed them my pocket-sized edition. "The absolute absence of the president is what you guys want? The only way to that kind of absence is death. Is that what you want? The resignation depends on me, the death is up to you guys. Or you want a medical team to declare me incapable of command and that finding to be upheld by the Supreme Court and the National Assembly? We no longer have either of those bodies, I wonder if you can find some doctors to do that for you anyway? That really isn't a viable option for you anyway, is it? So you are left with only one option, which I will tell you to make it easier, a constitutional alternative: separation of responsibility." Then I set an interpretive trap: I knew that they did not know much about the law, but there was a colonel there who was a lawyer and a good one. So I said to myself, "He is a lawyer and I am not, but he is not familiar with the constitution and I am."

Then I told him, "I can abandon my office, here is the constitution, shall we read it? 'Absolute absence of the president, this, that and the other, and abandonment of office.' " But the constitution says the National Assembly has to recognize the abandonment of office, and I did not read them that part. Then I said, "I am willing to sign a document that says I abandoned office, but not that I resigned." "But what is the difference?" the colonel asked, and then went out to talk on the telephone and came back with a borrowed copy of the constitution and then he realized what I was doing. "But, Chávez, the thing is that there is a problem: the National Assembly." "That is your problem, but it is the only way that I can sign that declaration, and you also have to let me use the phone, because if I am going to go to Mexico or to Cuba, I need to speak with the presidents of those countries. I am not going to leave here in a plane with no direction, and besides, I need to talk to my wife and kids, and settle a few other small things."

So then I started to draft a document that said "I, Hugo Chávez Frias, with such and such national ID number…" Of course, I wrote it in accordance with my plan: "Before the preponderance of the facts, I accept that I have been removed from office, and therefore I have abandoned it," something like that. And this guy took the bait and said to me, "Alright, I have to take them something signed."

So then they began to type up the document. The official who was writing was one of those I had been winning over—I had been talking with them one on one, most of them were decent guys—so he was typing slowly. He made a mistake and had to start over, I was still playing for time. The colonel told him to hurry up. Again, I noticed that the colonel was nervous. The area was filled with soldiers and I could see that some of them were taking up defensive positions, on alert for combat. So I called the admiral who was outside and I said to him, "What is the big threat here? Why are these guys taking out their rocket launchers and taking up defensive positions?" The guy nervously responds: "No, no, Mr. President, it is nothing, you know we have to protect your life."

I stayed in the room alone and the chief of my guard came up to me and whispered: "Mr. President, I did not sign anything," and then he disappeared. I stayed there wondering what was going on. I went to the bathroom to buy a bit more time and to come up with a strategy. Then I decided not to sign. I came out and I said: "Look, Lieutenant, don't keep writing that," and I said to the archbishop and the others, "I am definitely not going to sign anything, but thanks for your visit," and then I joked with them. "If you would like to stay here for the night in my luxurious jail, then you can leave in the morning. I have thought about it, and I am definitely not going to leave, my family is here, my kids, my party, and my people…. I don't know what is happening because you guys have not given me information or even a phone to call someone, you have kept me incommunicado."

It was really strange to me that they did not even try to resist what I told them, but instead quickly agreed: "OK, Chávez, you are right, we are leaving," and they quickly left. They were more nervous still when they came back five minutes later. The priest was the color of that white chair over there. The admiral comes up and says: "Mr. President, there is a situation here, a unit of paratroopers is on the way, they are about to arrive." He didn't know that a marine frigate and some Swift Boats were also coming. So I asked him why they were coming. "They are coming to rescue you." "And you, what are you thinking about doing about it?" "No, nothing, we are here to guard your life, nothing is going to happen, I spoke with General Baduel of the paratrooper unit and I told him to radio his helicopters and tell them that there is no resistance here, we are not going to fire a single shot." That sounded more like it, and I asked him, "And all of you guys, why did you stay?" "Because the plane that brought us has left already." I imagined that the plane heard over the radio that the attack helicopters were coming and decided to high-tail it out of there. I was laughing at this point, but I offered to take them off the island in my helicopter. The admiral came up to me again and told me I had a telephone call from the minister of defense. "I don't want to speak with that admiral—the one the coup conspirators had named minister of defense." "No, no, it is *your* minister of defense, Doctor Rangel." That got me very excited and I went to the phone. Just hearing the voice of José Vicente Rangel was like having the sun come out in the middle of the night. His voice was on fire. "Well, we are waiting for you. I will explain when you get here." "But where are you?" I asked. "Here in the Ministry of Defense, we have retaken the palace, and Carmona has been detained. The paratroopers are on their way to get you, they should arrive any minute and we are here waiting for your arrival, the people are waiting in the streets." "Have there been people killed?" "Well, a few, but we will explain everything when you get here." "And who are you with over there?" "With General López Hidalgo." "Let me have a word with him." And I spoke with him briefly: "Look, *compadre*, what's going on? Have many people been killed?" "No, Mr. President, don't worry, a few people were killed, but the people are in the streets and we control the army and the rest of the state power." "OK, I will see you soon."

Then I called the general in charge of the paratroopers in Mara-cay, which had been the bastion of resistance. I spoke with Baduel and Garcia Montoya who were at the command center. They explained a few things, but there was no time because the helicop-ters were already landing. There was no problem, and a few lawyers and doctors came to check up on me because there had been rumors that I had been beaten while in custody, and people had been worried about that.

Well, I think it was at about this time of the morning when they showed up [he looks at his watch and it is around 2:30 A.M.] because I got to the palace around 4 A.M. So that is why I told you I would remember this place for the rest of my life.

When I reflect on the April 11 coup, I remember the citation I mentioned earlier from JFK: "Those who make peaceful revolution impossible will make violent revolution inevitable." We chose to make our revolution constitutionally, through a constitutional process of unquestionable legitimacy. If at some point on April 11 or 12 I doubted that a democratic and peaceful revolution was possible, what happened on April 13 and 14—when an immense number of people came out into the streets, surrounding Miraflores and several army barracks, to demand my return—strongly reaffirmed my belief in that kind of revolution. Of course the battles are long and hard—we are talking about the art of making possible what appeared to many to be impossible.

Notes

CHAPTER 1

1   Ex-guerrilla commander, ex-director of the Venezuelan Communist party (PCV), who separated from the party to found the FALN-FLN (National Liberation Armed Forces–National Liberation Front), which became the PRV (Venezuelan Revolutionary party) and later, after dividing, became the PCV-Ruptura.

2   Agustín Blanco Muñoz, *Habla el Comandante,* Fundación Cátedra Pío Tamayo (Caracas: Universidad de Venezuela, third edition, 1998).

3   Muñoz, 122.

4   A U.S. military base where generations of Latin American military officials were trained. Many of them went on to use their training to torture and disappear members of left-wing factions in their home countries.

5   In Venezuela it is referred to as the Armed Force, not the Armed Forces. The Armed Force is composed of the army, navy, air force, and national guard.

6   Refers to the MBR 200.

7   Luis Bilbao, *Chávez y la Revolución Bolivariana* (Conversations with Luis Bilbao) (Buenos Aires: Ediciones Le Monde Diplomatique, 2002), 33.

8   Muñoz, 48–49. Federico Brito was a historian, university professor, and member of the PCV.

9   The Causa R began its incursion on Venezuela´s government in 1984 with four aldermen in Caroní, the most industrialized city in the state of Bolívar. Four years later the party won three national representatives and the following year they won control of the government in both Caroní and in the entire state of Bolívar. Three years after that, members of the Causa R were reelected to both those local governments, one of them was elected mayor of Caracas, and they obtained an absolute majority in the legislature. This notable electoral achievement seems to have contributed greatly to the fact that the people identify the Causa R with the Movimiento Bolivariano 200 led by Hugo Chávez. In the general elections of 1993 they increased their power from three to forty national representatives and eight senators. Nonetheless, for reasons which are beyond the scope of this book, they later lost control of both the state of Bolívar and of the city of Caracas. The Causa R claimed there was electoral fraud in both places. The truth seems to be more

complicated. In fact, the party fell apart after an unfortunate split in February of 1997. The then-secretary general, Lucas Mateo, and the high commander, Andrés Velásquez, with the support of the great majority of New Labor, led the group that kept the name the Causa R but had a more moderate line—accepting the wave of privatizations in the Orinoco region. Pablo Medina, an earlier secretary general, led the other group whose ranks included important members such as Aristóbulo Istúriz, the ex-mayor of Caracas, and Clemente Scotto, the ex-mayor of Caroní. They went on to form another party, the Homeland for All party (PPT), which supported Chávez in the 1998 presidential elections.

10 Director of the Causa R and currently of the PPT, minister of labor in the Chávez administration.

11 An ex-militant member of the PCV, founder of the Causa R and its main theorist. He died in 1982 at the age of forty-two. It was a deeply felt loss for his organization.

12 One of the founders of the Causa R, he was the secretary general for several years, deputy to the general assembly in 1993, and the founder and secretary general of the PPT when the Causa R split. Currently he has separated from the party and participates in the political front opposed to Chávez. He was involved with the coup on April 11, 2002.

13 A poor area to the west of Caracas that belongs to the parish of Sucre.

14 In an interview with García Márquez in 1999, Chávez revealed that there was a fourth captain—Rafael Baduel, who is currently the commander of the paratrooper base in Maracay.

15 Two months earlier, in conjunction with three soldiers and two sergeants, Chávez had formed a group called the Venezuelan People's Liberation Army, a group that didn't have any direction (Agustín Blanco Muñoz, op.cit., p. 57).

16 Lieutenant Colonel Francisco Arias Cárdenas was one of the founders of the Revolutionary Bolívarian Movement 200 (MBR 200). He played a role in the military uprising on February 4, 1992. After getting out of prison he separated himself from the movement, participated in the 1996 elections, and was elected governor of the state of Zulia. He is currently part of the opposition to the Chávez government, although after the April 11, 2002, military coup he accepted the president's call for dialogue and has continued to do so.

17 On February 27, 1989, there was a popular uprising in protest against a hike in the cost of public transportation and gas in Guarenas, in the state of Miranda. The price increases were a consequence of the neoliberal structural adjustment policies put into place by the then-president Carlos Andrés Pérez. In the face of brutal repression, the popular protests spread throughout all of Caracas.

18 A monument to a tree in Güere, a small town in the state of Aragua, where Simón Bolívar liked to rest 200 years ago.

19 Muñoz, 58.

20 Muñoz, 125.

21 Simón Rodríguez taught Bolívar and had a profound influence over his intellectual development.

22 Ezequiel Zamora was the leader of the liberals within the federal forces during the civil war from 1840 through 1850. He began an agrarian reform program that favored peasant farmers and he proved himself an ardent enemy of the landowning oligarchy. He firmly believed in civilian-military unity. He won remarkable victories in Los Llanos and was killed in the assault on San Carlos in 1860. As the hymn from the federal war said: "The oligarchy trembles, long live freedom!" His slogans included: "Free land and men," "Popular elections," and "War on the oligarchy."

23 Muñoz, 58.

24 An alliance between the Democratic Action party, COPEI, and URD, with the goal of sharing power among those parties.

25 A steelworker who was the secretary general of the Union of Industrial Steelworkers, and later governor of the state of Bolívar, one of the most industrialized in Venezuela; he represented the Causa R party as a presidential candidate in 1993. After the Causa R split, Velásquez, with the sector that kept the original party name, became part of the opposition to the Chávez government and recently formed part of the group that supported the April 2002 coup.

26 National Director of the Causa R and someone who has had a profound ideological and political influence on Andrés Velásquez.

27 A military uprising commanded by Hugo Chávez that sought to overthrow Carlos Andrés Pérez.

28 Guerrilla commander of the FALN and director of the PRV- Ruptura, who later became part of the Causa R and today is one of the directors of the PPT. He is also an expert on petroleum issues, ex-president of OPEC, and ex-president of PDVSA, currently minister of foreign relations.

29 The People's Electoral Movement, the third division of Democratic Action (AD). Its leader was Luis Beltrán Prieto Figueroa, an educator.

30 Rafael Caldera, the candidate put forward by the Convergencia party, a division of COPEI, won the 1993 presidential elections.

31 Current minister of education, culture, and sport.

32 While in the National Congress all the speakers from the AD and COPEI condemned the military rebellion. When David Morales Bello, the national director of the AD, arrived he started the slogan "death to the rebels." Caldera and Aristóbulo took a different position. They were critical of the system and they saw the military uprising as a consequence of the deterioration of the democratic regime. All these positions were widely known because the entire session was broadcast live on TV.

33 Caldera authorized an amnesty for the military prisoners who were involved in the February 4, 1992, rebellion.

34 Jorge Giordani, an economist who currently serves as the minister of planning and development, also a university professor.

35 Previously served as the minister of education, culture, and sport.

36 Currently the minister of finance, previously served as the minister of science and technology.

CHAPTER 2

1   The Venezuelan Government is divided into five branches: executive, legislative, judicial, electoral, and citizen. The moral branch consists of three institutions: the attorney general, the people's defender, and the national comptroller.

2   Members of MAS, who are now part of the opposition.

3   Director of the PPT, well-known journalist, and ex-director of the state's Channel 8.

4   Secretary general of the PPT.

5   Secretary general of the Confederation of Venezuelan Workers, equally involved in the coup.

6   A Venezuelan politician and member of the military. President of the Republic from 1941 to 1945. Sectors of the Left supported him and during his time in office he instituted policies such as agrarian reform, better contracts with U.S. oil companies, and the reestablishment of civil liberties.

7   The Causa R wanted to use us, and up to a point they were able to do it. They successfully won over Arias Cárdenas (one of the commanders of the February 1992 rebellion) that contributed to dividing the movement of the commanders.

8   Former mayor of the metropolitan area, one of Chávez's fiercest enemies.

9   Indeed the opposition, with the support of U.S. funding through the National Endowment for Democracy, did force a recall referendum on August 15, 2004. The election was certified by various international monitoring bodies including the Carter Center who reported 59.25 percent for Chávez and 40.74 percent against.

10 In order to amend the current Venezuelan constitution, the changes or articles must first be approved by the National Assembly and then submitted to a national referendum.

CHAPTER 3

1   Militant of the Acción Democrática party.

2   He is referring to a little school and medical center in Puerto Cruz.

3   Heinz Dietrich, *Hugo Chávez: Un nuevo proyecto latinoamericano* (Havana: Editorial de Ciencias Sociales, 2002), 31.

4   He refers to the video in which his resignation was announced and Carmona was installed as president.

5   Commander of the armored brigade of paratroopers of Valencia and currently serving as the commanding general of the army.

6   He refers to his visit to a poor neighborhood on June 20, 2002.

7   He refers to the section "La Respuesta de los Estados Unidos," paragraphs 31 to 36, particularly paragraph 32, of the book *La Izquierda en el Umbral del Siglo XXI. Haciendo Posible lo Imposible* by Marta Harnecker (Spain: Siglo XXI, third ed., 2000).

CHAPTER 4

1   At the third FTAA summit in Québec in April 2001.
2   Combustible fuel product patented by PDVSA that serves as a replacement for coal.
3   Dietrich, *Hugo Chávez*, 47.
4   Hugo Chávez, *Intervención sobre el Plan Extraordinario de Inversiones*, September 15, 2000, p. 4.

CHAPTER 5

1   Since July 8, 2004, Venezuela has been an associate member of Mercosur.

CHAPTER 6

1   The school at Puerto Cruz was inaugurated on June 13, 2002.
2   This controversial law was passed in the fall of 2004.
3   This island is located about 300 miles north of the Venezuelan coast, near the Virgin Islands.
4   The ex-vice minister of communication management, currently the director of information and public relations for the minister of the interior and justice.
5   State-owned and -run channel.
6   Minister of the Secretariat of the president.
7   Achieved with governors from all over the country, including some from the opposition.
8   Federation of artisans, small, medium, and large Venezuelan industries.
9   National Industrial Federation.
10 Venezuelan Industrial Confederation.

CHAPTER 7

1   Chávez created the Revolutionary Political Command to direct the revolutionary process. Its forty-one members, drawn from a range of sympathetic parties (MVR, PPT, PCV, MEP, MAS, Socialist League) and civil society groups (FBT, FBM, FBC) were sworn in on January 10, 2002.
2   Hugo Chávez, *Juramentación del Comando de la Revolución en la Sala Plenaria del Parque Central de Caracas*, Venezolana de Televisión (VTV), Caracas, January 10, 2002.
3   The part of the MAS that continues to support Chávez.
4   After the military coup on April 11, 2002, and the death threats he received, the president's security suggested that he restrict his public appearances. Therefore, for a couple of months he spent very little time in the streets. One young official told me, "The security are worse than fascists, they are separating the president from his people when his strength is derived from that fluid contact he has maintained with the popular sectors of society."

5   General Jorge García Carneiro, chief of the Third Infantry Division, one of the
    generals who defended Chávez during the 2002 coup. He is now minister of
    defense.

CHAPTER 8

1   Now his ex-wife.
2   He is referring to the decree with which Carmona appointed himself president
    and dissolved the branches of government: the Supreme Court, the attorney
    general, the people's defender, the national comptroller, the National Electoral
    Council, and the existing executive branch.

Notes

A

abandonment of office, 184–85; and resignation, 89–90, 94, 96–97, 179, 181–85

abstention, 45, 60

AD party (Acción Democrática Party), 17, 50, 53, 58, 154, 190n32

agriculture, 175

Air Force, 37, 75. *See also* military

ALBA (Bolivarian Alliance of the Americas), 113, 120–21

Allende, Salvador, 26–27, 56, 137, 144

alliance, 42, 50–51, 69, 127–28, 138; civilian-military, 73–78, 81–82; *Polo Patrótico*, 18, 62

Alliance for Progress, 103

Aló presidente (radio and tv program), 12, 147, 148–53, 171

aluminum, 122

Alvarado, Juan Velasco, 27

amendments, 126; by referendum, 71–72

Amin, Samir, 132

El antichavismo y la estupidex ilustrada (Lander), 141

Arcay, Jacinto Pérez, 24

Argentina, 113

Armed Forces, 20, 21

army, 24. *See also* military

Army as an Agent of Social Change, The (El ejército como agente de cambio social) (Héller), 24

artillery, 122; and weapons, 45, 83, 88

Attorney General's office, 65–66, 70

B

Baduel, Raul, 19, 98, 186

Bandera Roja guerrillas, 29, 36–37

banking, 18, 81, 109–11, 112, 115, 177

Banzer, Hugo, 124

Barranco Yopal project, 75

Bernal, Fredy, 17, 170

Blair, Tony, 128

Bolívar, Simón, 39, 54, 106, 120–22

Bolivarian Alliance of the Americas

(ALBA), 120–21

Bolivarian Army 200, 31

Bolivarianism, 9, 12–13, 21, 106, 169; circles in, 19, 158, 160–63; committees in, 38, 43, 158; in Military Academy, 25–26

Bolivarian Revolutionary Movement. *See* MBR 200

Bolivia, 124

G

H

I

P

R

S

T